Italian

Everyday Cookbook

STAR
FIRE

This is a Star Fire book
First published in 2006

06 08 10 09 07

1 3 5 7 9 10 8 6 4 2

Star Fire is part of
The Foundry Creative Media Company Limited
Crabtree Hall, Crabtree Lane, Fulham, London, SW6 6TY

Visit our website: www.star-fire.co.uk

ISBN-10: 1-84451-009-3 ISBN-13: 978-1-84451-009-2

The CIP record for this book is available from the British Library.

Printed in China

ACKNOWLEDGEMENTS

Publisher and Creative Director: Nick Wells
Project Editor and Editorial: Sarah Goulding
Design and Production: Chris Herbert, Mike Spender, Colin Rudderham and Claire Walker

Authors: Catherine Atkinson, Juliet Barker, Gina Steer, Vicki Smallwood,
Carol Tennant, Mari Mererid Williams, Elizabeth Wolf-Cohen and Simone Wright
Editorial: Gina Steer and Karen Fitzpatrick
Photography: Colin Bowling, Paul Forrester and Stephen Brayne
Home Economists and Stylists: Jacqueline Bellefontaine,
Mandy Phipps, Vicki Smallwood and Penny Stephens

All props supplied by Barbara Stewart at Surfaces

NOTE
Recipes using uncooked eggs should be avoided by infants,
the elderly, pregnant women and anyone suffering from an illness.

Contents

Soups & Starters

Fish

Meats

Poultry & Game

Vegetables

Desserts

Hygiene in the Kitchen

It is important to remember that many foods can carry some form of bacteria. In most cases, the worst it will lead to is a bout of food poisoning or gastroenteritis, although for certain people this can be serious. The risk can be reduced or eliminated, however, by good hygiene and proper cooking.

Do not buy food that is past its sell-by date and do not consume food that is past its use-by date. When buying food, use the eyes and nose. If the food looks tired, limp or a bad colour or it has a rank, acrid or simply bad smell, do not buy or eat it under any circumstances.

Take special care when preparing raw meat and fish. A separate chopping board should be used for each, and the knife, board and your hands should be thoroughly washed before handling or preparing any other food.

Regularly clean, defrost and clear out the refrigerator or freezer – it is worth checking the packaging to see exactly how long each product is safe to freeze. Avoid handling food if suffering from an upset stomach as bacteria can be passed on through food preparation.

Dish cloths and tea towels must be washed and changed regularly. Ideally use disposable cloths which should be replaced on a daily basis. More durable cloths should be left to soak in bleach, then washed in the washing machine at a high temperature.

Keep your hands, cooking utensils and food preparation surfaces clean and do not allow pets to climb on to any work surfaces.

Buying

Avoid bulk buying where possible, especially fresh produce such as meat, poultry, fish, fruit and vegetables. Fresh foods lose their nutritional value rapidly, so buying a little at a time minimises loss of nutrients. It also means your fridge won't be so full, which reduces the effectiveness of the refrigeration process.

When buying prepackaged goods such as cans or pots of cream and yogurts, check that the packaging is intact and not damaged or pierced at all. Cans should not be dented, pierced or rusty. Check the sell-by dates even for cans and packets of dry ingredients such as flour and rice. Store fresh foods in the refrigerator as soon as possible – not in the car or the office.

When buying frozen foods, ensure that they are not heavily iced on the outside and that the contents feel completely frozen. Ensure that the frozen foods have been stored in the cabinet at the correct storage level and the temperature is below -18°C/-0.4°F. Pack in cool bags to transport home and place in the freezer as soon as possible after purchase.

Preparation

Make sure that all work surfaces and utensils are clean and dry. Hygiene should be given priority at all times. Separate chopping boards should be used for raw and cooked meats, fish and vegetables. Currently, a variety of good quality plastic boards come in various designs and colours. This makes differentiating easier and the plastic has the added hygienic advantage of being washable at high temperatures in the dishwasher. If using the board for fish, first wash in cold water, then in hot to prevent odour. Also remember that knives and utensils should always be thoroughly cleaned after use.

When cooking, be particularly careful to keep cooked and raw food separate to avoid any contamination. It is worth washing all fruits and vegetables regardless of whether they are going to be eaten raw or lightly cooked.

This rule should apply even to prewashed herbs and salads.

Do not reheat food more than once. If using a microwave, always check that the food is piping hot all the way through – in theory, the food should reach 70°C/158°F and needs to be cooked at that temperature for at least three minutes to ensure that all bacteria are killed.

All poultry must be thoroughly thawed before using, including chicken and poussin. Remove the food to be thawed from the freezer and place in a shallow dish to contain the juices. Leave the food in the refrigerator until it is completely thawed. A 1.4 kg/3 lb whole chicken will take about 26–30 hours to thaw. To speed up the process, immerse the chicken in cold water, making sure that the water is changed regularly. When the joints can move freely and no ice crystals remain in the cavity, the bird is completely thawed.

Once thawed, remove the wrapper and pat the chicken dry. Place the chicken in a shallow dish, cover lightly and store as close to the base of the refrigerator as possible. The chicken should be cooked as soon as possible.

Some foods can be cooked from frozen including many prepacked foods such as soups, sauces, casseroles and breads. Where applicable follow the manufacturers' instructions.

Vegetables and fruits can also be cooked from frozen, but meats and fish should be thawed first. The only time food can be refrozen is when the food has been thoroughly thawed then cooked. Once the food has cooled then it can be frozen again, but it should only be stored for one month.

All poultry and game (except for duck) must be cooked thoroughly. When cooked, the juices will run clear on the thickest part of the bird – the best area to try is usually the thigh. Other meats, like minced meat and pork should be cooked right the way through. Fish should turn opaque, be firm in texture and break easily into large flakes.

When cooking leftovers, make sure they are reheated until piping hot and that any sauce or soup reaches boiling point first.

Storing, Refrigerating and Freezing

Meat, poultry, fish, seafood and dairy products should all be refrigerated. The temperature of the refrigerator should be between 1–5°C/34–41°F while the freezer temperature should not rise above -18°C/-0.4°F.

To ensure the optimum refrigerator and freezer temperature, avoid leaving the door open for long periods of time.

Try not to overstock the refrigerator as this reduces the airflow inside and therefore the effectiveness in cooling the food within.

When refrigerating cooked food, allow it to cool down quickly and completely before refrigerating. Hot food will raise the temperature of the refrigerator and possibly affect or spoil other food stored in it.

Food within the refrigerator and freezer should always be covered. Raw and cooked food should be stored in separate parts of the refrigerator. Cooked food should be kept on the top shelves of the refrigerator, while raw meat, poultry and fish should be placed on bottom shelves to avoid drips and cross-contamination. It is recommended that eggs should be refrigerated in order to maintain their freshness and shelf life.

Take care that frozen foods are not stored in the freezer for too long. Blanched vegetables can be stored for one month; beef, lamb, poultry and pork for six months and unblanched vegetables and fruits in syrup for a year. Oily fish and sausages should be stored for three months. Dairy products can last four to six months, while cakes and pastries should be kept in the freezer for three to six months.

High Risk Foods

Certain foods may carry risks to people who are considered vulnerable such as the elderly, the ill, pregnant women, babies, young infants and those suffering from a recurring illness.

It is advisable to avoid those foods listed below which belong to a higher-risk category.

There is a slight chance that some eggs carry the bacteria salmonella. Cook the eggs until both the yolk and the white are firm to eliminate this risk. Pay particular attention to dishes and products incorporating lightly cooked or raw eggs which should be eliminated from the diet. Hollandaise sauce, mayonnaise, mousses, soufflés and meringues all use raw or lightly cooked

eggs, as do custard-based dishes, ice creams and sorbets. These are all considered high-risk foods to the vulnerable groups mentioned above.

Certain meats and poultry also carry the potential risk of salmonella and so should be cooked thoroughly until the juices run clear and there is no pinkness left. Unpasteurised products such as milk, cheese (especially soft cheese), pâté, meat (both raw and cooked) all have the potential risk of listeria and should be avoided.

When buying seafood, buy from a reputable source which has a high turnover to ensure freshness. Fish should have bright clear eyes, shiny skin and bright pink or red gills. The fish should feel stiff to the touch, with a slight smell of sea air and iodine. The flesh of fish steaks and fillets should be translucent with no signs of discolouration. Molluscs such as scallops, clams and mussels are sold fresh and are still alive. Avoid any that are open or do not close when tapped lightly. In the same way, univalves such as cockles or winkles should withdraw back into their shells when lightly prodded. When choosing cephalopods such as squid and octopus they should have a firm flesh and pleasant sea smell.

As with all fish, whether it is shellfish or seafish, care is required when freezing it. It is imperative to check whether the fish has been frozen before. If it has been frozen, then it should not be frozen again under any circumstances.

Fresh Ingredients

Italian cuisine is popular all over the world and basic Italian storecupboard ingredients are commonplace items on supermarket shelves. Even fresh ingredients that used to be difficult to find are available all year round, often in parts of the world where previously they were unheard of. For those who enjoy Italian food and cooking this is good news – delicious, authentic Italian cuisine can now be enjoyed anywhere and at any time.

Cheeses

Dolcelatte This cheese, which translates as 'sweet milk', comes from the Lombardy region. Dolcelatte is a creamy, blue cheese and has a luscious, sweet taste. It is very soft and melts in the mouth, often appealing to those who find more traditional blue cheeses, like Roquefort and Gorgonzola, too strongly flavoured.

Fontina This is a dense, smooth and slightly elastic cheese with a straw-coloured interior. Fontina is made in the Valle d'Aosta region and has a delicate nutty flavour with a hint of mild honey. It is often served melted in which case the flavour becomes very earthy.

Gorgonzola This is a traditional blue cheese from the Lombardy region. Made from cow's milk, the cheese has a sharp, spicy flavour as well as being rich and creamy.

Mascarpone Technically, mascarpone is not a cheese but a by-product obtained from making Parmesan. A culture is added to the cream that has been skimmed off the milk that was used to make the cheese. This is then gently heated and allowed to mature and thicken. Mascarpone is most famous as the main ingredient in Tiramisu, but it is a very versatile ingredient and is used in all sorts of sweet and savoury recipes.

Mozzarella di Bufala Mozzarella is a fresh cheese, prized more for its texture than its flavour which is really quite bland. Mozzarella cheese melts beautifully, however, on pizzas and in pasta dishes, and is also good served cold in salads. It is usually sold in tubs along with its whey and should have a floppy rather than a rubbery texture. The fresher it is when eaten, the better.

Parmigiano-Reggiano One of the world's finest cheeses, Parmigiano-Reggiano is also one of the most versatile cooking cheeses. Its production is very carefully regulated to guarantee a consistent high-quality result. The trademark is branded all over the rind, so that even a small piece is easily identified. Buy it in pieces, rather than ready-grated.

Pecorino This is the generic term for cheeses made purely from sheep's milk. All Pecorino cheeses are excellent for grating or shaving on to both hot and cold dishes. Each type of Pecorino is characteristic of a particular region and a particular breed of sheep. Pecorino Romano is made in the countryside around Rome between November and late June. Pecorino Sardo is made in Sardinia and Pecorino Toscano comes from Tuscany and tends to mature younger than other Pecorino cheeses.

Ricotta When cheese is made, the solids in the milk are separated from the liquid by coagulation, however, some solids are always lost to the whey. To retrieve these solids, the milk is heated until they come to the surface. They then are skimmed off and drained in woven baskets until the curd is solid enough to stick together. The resulting cheese is ricotta (literally meaning 'recooked'). Good-quality ricotta should be firm but not solid and consist of fine, delicate grains. Ricotta is used in both savoury and sweet dishes.

Cured Meats

Coppa This boned shoulder of pork is rolled and cured with salt, pepper and nutmeg and then aged for about three months. It has a flavour not unlike prosciutto but contains equal amounts of fat and lean. It is excellent for larding the breasts of game birds, adding both fat and flavour, or for wrapping leaner types of meats.

Pancetta Essentially, pancetta is Italian streaky bacon but its depth of flavour is unrivalled by ordinary bacon. It is often flavoured with herbs, cloves, nutmeg, garlic, salt and pepper and sometimes fennel seeds – it is then often air-dried. It is also available smoked. Use it in slices or cut into lardons.

Prosciutto There are many types of cured ham available, but the two best types are Prosciutto di San Daniele and Prosciutto di Parma. The first comes from the Friuli region where the pigs feed in the fields and oak woods, accounting for the leanness of the meat. The second type, also known as Parma ham or prosciutto crudo, is made from pigs that have been fed on local grain as well as the whey left over from the making of Parmigiano-Reggiano. This meat is usually fattier.

Salami Italy produces a huge range of salamis, each with its own local character. The one most commonly available in Britain is probably Milano salami which comes sliced in packets or in one piece from major supermarkets.

Vegetables and Herbs

Artichokes Very popular in Italian cooking, artichokes are available in many different varieties and forms: from tiny, young artichokes cooked and eaten whole to enormous globe artichokes, prized for their meaty hearts which can be sliced, stuffed or grilled. Artichokes are often cooked and preserved and served as an antipasto, on pizzas or in pasta dishes.

Aubergines These vegetables are popular all over the Mediterranean, probably because of their affinity with olive oil and garlic. In Britain, aubergines tend to be fatter and somewhat juicier than the Mediterranean varieties which are often elongated and marked with bright purple streaks.

Broad Beans Fresh broad beans are a prized early-summer speciality and in Italy are eaten raw with pecorino cheese. As the season progresses, they are best cooked and peeled as they tend to become coarse and grainy.

Cavallo Nero A member of the cabbage family, cavallo nero has long, slender, very ridged leaves which are dark green in colour. It has a strong but rather sweet cabbage flavour. Large supermarkets stock it in season, but if it is unavailable, use Savoy cabbage instead.

Garlic Garlic is one of the most important flavours in Italian cooking. When buying garlic, check it carefully – the heads should be firm without soft spots. Look for fresh, green garlic in spring.

Herbs A number of fresh herbs are used in Italian cooking but the most important ones are basil, parsley, rosemary, sage, marjoram and

oregano. These are all widely used herbs and are available from most supermarkets but are also very easy to grow, even on a windowsill.

Lemons Italian lemons tend to be a little sweeter than the ones available in Britain. They are an essential flavour in many Italian dishes, especially seafood and sweet dishes.

Pumpkins and Squashes Often overlooked in Britain, pumpkins and the many varieties of squash are widely used in Italian cooking. They are excellent for enriching stews – some varieties have flesh which breaks down during cooking. They are also used for risottos and pasta fillings. Pumpkins and squashes and have an affinity with prosciutto, sage, pine nuts, Parmesan cheese and mostardo di cremona (see the Dry Ingredients section).

Rocket This peppery salad leaf has become popular in recent years and is now very easy to find. It is known by many other names including rucola, rughetta, arugula and roquette. It does not keep well.

Tomatoes Tomatoes are another essential flavour in Italian recipes. Unfortunately, British tomatoes tend not to be as good as their Italian counterparts. It is best to use tomatoes only in season and, at other times, to use good-quality, tinned Italian tomatoes.

Wild Mushrooms Mushroom hunting is a very popular and lucrative business in Italy, so much so that there are strict regulations regarding the minimum size for picking mushrooms. Many excellent edible varieties of wild mushrooms grow in Britain, but it is vital to seek expert advice before picking them on your own as some varieties are poisonous. Many large supermarkets now sell varieties of wild mushrooms in season but they tend to be expensive.

Bread

Italian breads tend to be coarser and more open-textured than British breads. They are made with unbleached flours and are left to prove for longer so that the flavour develops fully. Italian breads also tend to have a crustier exterior. Look out for Pugliese and ciabatta breads. Foccacia, a soft-crusted bread, is also popular and can be flavoured with herbs, sun-dried tomatoes or garlic.

Seafood

Italy has a large coastline relative to its size and, as a result, seafood is a very popular choice. A huge variety of fish and shellfish are available, and large meals such as those served at weddings or other special celebrations will always include a fish course.

Meat, Poultry and Game

Italians are amongst the world's greatest meat eaters. Most meals will be based on meat of some kind. Popular choices include beef, chicken, pork and lamb but duck, guinea fowl, pheasant, pigeon, rabbit, veal and many kinds of offal are also used.

Dry Ingredients

As with fresh ingredients, many items previously unavailable have, in recent years, appeared on supermarket and delicatessen shelves. Many dry ingredients keep well and are worth stocking up on.

Amaretti Biscuits These delicious, little crisp biscuits are made from almonds and most closely resemble macaroons. They come individually wrapped in beautiful paper and are good to eat on their own or with a sweet dessert wine. They are also useful as ingredients in desserts as they add crunch and flavour.

Anchovies These come in several forms and are an essential Italian ingredient. Anchovies can be treated almost as a seasoning in many recipes. Salted anchovies are sold in bottles and must be rinsed thoroughly to remove the excess salt. If the anchovies are whole, remove the heads and bones before using. If they are preserved in oil, remove them from the oil and drain them on absorbent kitchen paper. Some recipes require that anchovies are soaked in milk for 10–15 minutes (this makes the fillets less salty and less oily). By doing so the anchovies will simply melt on cooking. Do not soak the anchovies in milk if the fillets are to be used uncooked as in salads, for example.

Bottarga This is the salted and sun-dried roe of either grey mullet or tuna. It is available from Italian delicatessens or speciality shops (tuna bottarga is

less delicately flavoured). Spaghetti with mullet bottarga, olive oil and chilli flakes is listed on every restaurant menu in Sardinia. Bottarga can also be finely shaved into a salad of raw fennel, lemon juice and olive oil.

Candied Peel Citrus fruit plays an important part in Italian cooking. Candied peel is found in all sorts of desserts. Buy it whole and chop it finely for the best flavour.

Canned Tomatoes As the British climate does not produce an abundance of outdoor grown, sun-ripened tomatoes, good-quality, tinned Italian plum tomatoes are the next best thing for making sauces. The fruit should be deep red and the liquid should be thick and not watery. Buy them whole or chopped.

Capers The flower buds of a bush native to the Mediterranean, capers are available both salted and preserved in vinegar. Small capers generally have a better flavour than larger ones. When using salted capers, it is important to soak and rinse them to remove the excess salt. Those preserved in vinegar should be drained and rinsed before use.

Coffee Italians prefer dark, roasted coffee and they pioneered the drinking of cappuccino and espresso. It is best to buy whole beans, as freshly roasted as possible, and grind them yourself as needed.

Dried Herbs These days, most recipes call for fresh herbs but dried herbs still have their place. Oregano dries particularly well and has a much less astringent flavour when dried; it is essential in tomato sauces. Other herbs that dry well are rosemary, sage and thyme. Dried basil, however, is no substitute for fresh.

Dried Mushrooms The most commonly available – and most affordable – type of dried mushroom is porcini. They are usually sold in 10 g packets which is generally plenty for one or two recipes and should be soaked in almost boiling water or stock for 20–30 minutes, until tender. Carefully squeeze out any excess liquid – it will still be hot – and then chop as needed. Reserve the liquor as it contains a great deal of flavour. It is wise, however, to strain it before use as it can contain grit.

Dried Pulses Pulses are an excellent source of carbohydrate and also contain protein, making them particularly useful to vegetarians. Dried pulses should all be treated in the same way – soak them overnight in plenty of water (2 to 3 times their volume), then drain and cover with fresh water. Bring to the boil and boil hard for 10 minutes, reduce the temperature and simmer gently, until tender (check packet instructions for full cooking times). Do not add salt to dried pulses until they are cooked as salt will make the skins tough. Italians make use of a large number of different types of pulses and lentils.

Cannellini Beans These beans are long and slender with a creamy texture. Cannellini beans take up other flavours very well, especially garlic, herbs and olive oil.

Borlotti Beans These are large, rounded beans which cook to a uniform brown colour. They also have a creamy texture and are very good in soups and stews.

Broad Beans These are available dried; either whole, with skins or split. The whole ones are excellent in soups. The split beans are popular in Eastern European countries, as well as Greece and Turkey where they are used in dishes such as falafel.

Chickpeas *Ceci* in Italian, chickpeas were introduced from the Middle East. Look out for big ones when buying them dry. They are excellent in soups and also in vegetable dishes. Chickpeas need a long cooking time.

Lentils Look for Lentilles de Puy. Although not Italian, these lentils are possibly the best flavoured of the lentil family. They are small and beautifully coloured from green-brown to blue. They also hold their shape well when cooked, making them easy to serve as a side dish – simply dress with olive oil. Similar lentils named Castelluccio are also grown in Umbria. They are also small but paler green in colour. Lentils are traditionally served with Bollito Misto, a famous New Year's Eve dish consisting of various meats, lentils and mostarda di cremona (see below).

Flour In most Italian recipes where flour is required, plain flour can easily be substituted. However, when making pizza or pasta dough, look for Tipo '00' flour which is very fine and very strong, making it ideal for these two dishes. If you cannot find it, use strong bread flour instead.

Mostarda di cremona Also known as mostarda di frutta, it is made of candied fruits such as peaches, apricots, pears, figs and cherries which are preserved in a honey, white wine and mustard syrup. It is available from large supermarkets and specialist shops.

Nuts Almonds, hazelnuts, walnuts and pistachios are all popular in Italian cooking, particularly in dessert recipes. Buy from a supplier with a quick turnover to guarantee that the nuts are fresh.

Olives Olives grow all over Italy and are synonymous with Italian cooking. Olives are available in most supermarkets, although it is worth looking for them in specialist shops that might preserve them with more interesting flavours. If you are lucky enough to find fresh olives, soak them in a very strong brine for a couple of weeks, then rinse them and preserve in oil and flavourings of your choice.

Panettone Generally available around Christmas, panettone is a sweet bread enriched with egg and butter, similar to French brioche. It is usually flavoured with candied citrus fruits although it can be plain. It keeps very well and is delicious toasted and spread with butter or used in bread and butter pudding.

Pine Nuts An essential ingredient in pesto sauce, pine nuts are found in all sorts of Italian recipes, both savoury and sweet. They are widely available and are delicious toasted and tossed in with pasta. They burn very easily, however, and are relatively expensive, so take care when toasting.

Raisins Italy is a large grape-producing nation so, not surprisingly, raisins feature alongside citrus fruits in many recipes. Look for plump, juicy looking fruit and try to buy only what you need as raisins can become sugary if kept for too long.

Semolina Not to be confused with the semolina used in puddings, semola di grano duro is flour from Italian durum wheat. This produces a granular-textured flour as opposed to finer-textured flour used in breadmaking. Large supermarkets and Italian delicatessens sell semola di grano duro, but if it is unavailable, use strong bread flour instead.

Sun-dried Tomatoes Although they seem ubiquitous now, sun-dried tomatoes were unavailable outside Italy until the end of the 1980s. Sun-dried tomatoes are ripe plum tomatoes which have been dried in the sun. Often they have been rehydrated by being soaked in water and then preserved in oil. To use them, simply drain them on absorbent kitchen paper and chop as necessary. Also available now are semi-dried tomatoes, which have a sweeter, fresher flavour and a softer, less leathery texture. If you find sun-dried tomatoes which are not in oil, put them into a bowl and cover with boiling water. Leave for about 30 minutes, or until softened, before using.

Sun-dried Tomato Purée As the name suggests, this a paste made from sun-dried tomatoes. Use it in the same way as you would tomato purée. Sometimes it has other flavours added, such as garlic or herbs, in which case it can be used in salad dressings or mixed with pesto to dress pasta.

Pasta, Rice and Polenta

Pasta

Throughout the world, Italian cooking is perceived to be synonymous with pasta. Of course, the Italians cook with many more ingredients than pasta alone, but, it is without a doubt one of the most popular carbohydrates. Pasta comes in a bewildering variety of shapes, and commercial companies are constantly coming up with new and ever more imaginative ideas for new types of pasta.

Choosing the correct shape of pasta is not necessarily the tricky exercise that it first appears. Creamy, thick or chunky sauces need the support of sturdier, thicker shapes like bows, tubes or shells. Oil-based sauces are best with long, thin pasta such as spaghetti or linguine.

Most dried pasta is simply made from flour and water which is shaped and allowed to dry. Sometimes the dough will have been enriched with egg, in which case the packet will say all' uovo. These pastas have a richer flavour than those made without eggs and may be more expensive.

Also available dried are flavoured pastas. Spinach and tomato are very popular but pastas flavoured with squid ink, wild mushrooms, herbs, chillies and garlic are also available. When buying or making a sauce to accompany these pastas, choose carefully as their flavour is subtle and may be overpowered by strong flavours.

Fresh pasta is sold in almost all supermarkets and is also available flavoured. Again, spinach and tomato are the most common flavours. Filled pastas are also very useful as they usually require very simple sauces to set them off – a little melted butter, some grated Parmesan cheese and some freshly ground black pepper may be all that is needed.

More adventurous cooks may want to try making their own fresh pasta. The recipe is very simple, consisting essentially of just flour and eggs, but achieving a dough that is neither too wet and sticky, nor too dry and flaky, is a bit more tricky. It will usually take one or two attempts to get it right.

There are a number of methods of mixing and kneading the dough: by hand, in a food processor or food mixer, or using a pasta machine.

Fresh Pasta Basic Recipe

225 g/8 oz Italian type 'oo'
flour, semola di grano duro or
strong plain flour
2 large eggs, plus 1 egg yolk
1 tbsp olive oil
½ tsp salt

By Hand

Put the flour in a mound on a clean work surface or table. Make a well in the centre of the mound, leaving high sides so the egg cannot escape. Break in the eggs and add the egg yolk, olive oil and salt. With a fork at first, and then with your hands, draw the flour into the liquid gradually, until the mixture forms a rough paste. Add more flour if the mixture is very sticky and add a little water if it is too dry.

At this stage, begin kneading the dough with the heel of your hand for about 10 minutes until the dough is smooth and elastic. It will feel like soft leather. If it is at all sticky, knead in a little more flour. If it is not elastic, add a touch of water. Wrap the dough in clingfilm and leave to rest for at least 30 minutes. At this stage, the dough can be frozen for up to four weeks. Do not leave the dough in the refrigerator for more than a few hours or the surface will oxidise and dark specks will appear. These are not harmful but they are unattractive.

By Food Processor or Food Mixer

Put all the ingredients into the bowl of a food processor fitted with a plastic mixing blade or a food mixer fitted with kneading hooks. In the food processor, mix together the ingredients using the pulse button until the mixture begins to form a ball on the blade. Turn the machine on and allow it to knead the dough until it is smooth and elastic – this may take about 5 minutes and you may need to hold on to the machine to keep it from jumping around. In a food mixer, on a low speed, mix the ingredients together, scraping down the bowl occasionally, then increase the speed and knead for about 10 minutes, until the dough is smooth and elastic. Reserve as above.

Pasta Machine

Mix the dough using one of the earlier methods until the dough comes together. Feed the dough through the rollers of a pasta machine on its widest setting. Fold the dough in half and repeat. Keep repeating until the dough is smooth and elastic. Reserve as earlier. (The dough can be rolled using a rolling pin, but it takes a great deal of skill and patience to roll the dough finely this way.) Unwrap the rested dough and divide into eight pieces. With the pasta machine on its widest setting, flatten the first piece of dough and pass

through the rollers. Decrease the setting by one notch and feed the dough through again. Continue decreasing and rolling until the dough has passed through the finest setting. Hang the sheet of pasta over a clean broom handle suspended between two chairs or on a pasta drying rack. Repeat with the remaining dough. The dough is now ready to be cut or filled as required.

Flavoured pasta

Many flavourings can be added to the basic pasta dough with varying results. The best results are obtained by using strongly flavoured ingredients such as spinach, tomato, saffron, squid ink, fresh herbs or cocoa powder. The dough should have the same consistency as unflavoured dough and may require more flour or liquid to achieve the same result.

Spinach Pasta Add 75 g/3 oz of cooked, drained and puréed spinach along with approximately 50 g/2 oz of flour to the basic recipe. You may need a little more or less flour to make the dough smooth.

Tomato Pasta Add 2 tablespoons of tomato purée or sun-dried tomato purée to the basic recipe along with approximately 100 g/3½ oz of flour.

Saffron Pasta Soak a large pinch of crushed saffron strands in 1 tablespoon of hot water for 1 minute. Replace one of the eggs in the basic recipe with this mixture.

Squid Ink Pasta Add the ink of 2 squid (or one packet of squid ink from a fishmonger) along with an extra 100 g/ 3½ oz of flour (less if using packet ink) to the basic recipe.

Fresh Herbs There are two ways to add fresh herbs to pasta. The first is to add very finely chopped leaves to the basic dough and proceed as in the basic recipe. The second is to add whole leaves during the final rolling stage; pass the dough through the widest two notches on the pasta machine, lay whole leaves over one half of the dough and fold the other half over to enclose. Pass through the second notch again then carry on rolling as in the basic recipe. The herbs will be encased in the dough, and when stretched, will be visible as pretty green streaks in the finished dough. It may not be possible to pass this dough through the finest setting on the pasta machine.

Chocolate Pasta Replace 3 tablespoons of the flour with sifted, unsweetened cocoa powder and proceed as in the basic recipe. This type of pasta is often served in Italy with game sauces.

Rice

Rice is a surprisingly common ingredient in Italian cooking, especially in dishes originating in the north of Italy where most of the rice is grown. The most popular rice dish in Italy is risotto, which at its best is haute cuisine, but even when mediocre is still the finest comfort food around.

There are three main types of risotto rice available in Britain: Arborio, vialone nano and carnaroli. They differ slightly in quality with carnaroli being the best and arborio being the cheapest. They also differ slightly in starch content which makes each of them suited to different recipes. This difference, however, is really only detectable to an expert palate. In practice, all of the risotto rices are interchangeable. Buy the best you can afford.

All risotto rices are short-grain with a very high starch content.

As the risotto is stirred during cooking, the starch is released and produces the creamy texture typical of risotto. The rice should be cooked until 'al dente' so that it is cooked through, but still has a little bite to it.

There are some simple rules for making risotto. Firstly, keep the stock hot so that when adding it to the rice it does not interrupt the cooking process and secondly, add more stock only when the rice has absorbed the previous ladleful. Do not add cheese to a seafood-based risotto. Most risottos benefit from the addition of a knob of butter stirred in just at the end.

Polenta

Polenta appears on just about every fashionable restaurant menu nowadays. Polenta is ground maize meal. The texture is grainy and the colour should be a deep orangey-yellow. It should smell of simmering fresh corn.

Polenta can be served either wet (freshly cooked polenta) or set (cooled cooked polenta cut into shapes and grilled). When the polenta is wet, it is best served with dishes which have a lot of juices – the polenta will soak up the juices and take on their flavour. When grilled, it has a crust with a soft interior that is good with sauces as well as with salads or braised vegetables. Try adding butter, cheese, fresh herbs, cooked mushrooms or chopped sun-dried tomatoes to polenta which can otherwise seem bland to an uninitiated palate.

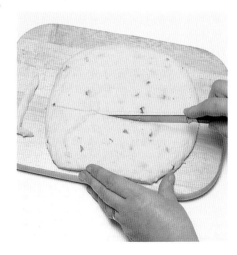

Wine, Olive Oil and Vinegars

Wine

Italy has long been a major wine-producing country but the classification system put into place in the 1960s was both confusing and misleading. For example, a wine labelled as vino da tavola (table wine) could, under the former system, vary in quality from the very worst example to the finest wine with nothing on the label to distinguish it to the non-discerning buyer. Recently, the classification system has been reworked in accordance with the French system so as to reflect the quality of the wine rather than to emphasise the method of production, which can often be based on expediency rather than quality.

Italian wines are produced specifically to accompany food. Many modern Italian wines are very fine and worth seeking out. Italy produces a huge range of unique wines, often using varieties of grapes only grown there, but also using well-known varieties grown all over the world. Reds, whites, sparkling and fortified wines are all produced in Italy, and some of the most noted examples are as follows.

Red Wines

The three most important grapes in Italian wine production are Nebbiolo, Montepulciano and Sangiovese. Nebbiolo is the grape used to produce Barolo and Barbaresco as well as some less well-known wines. Young wines made with this grape tend to be very harsh with high levels of tannin and acidity, but once aged, can become remarkably rich with chocolate, raisin, prune, tobacco and woodsmoke flavours.

Montepulciano is the grape found in Montepulciano d'Abruzzo DOC. Good examples are citrus-fresh and plummily rich, tannic, ripe and slightly sour.

Sangiovese is the grape of Chianti.

Chianti and wines in the style of Chianti have had a reputation for being rather thin and dull. This was because the former regulations allowed the wine producers to add a high percentage of white juice – up to one third – which meant that the wine was weak even before it was bottled.

In recent years, however, there has been a return to using original Tuscan rootstock vines, which have a lower yield than the vines planted in the 1970s, but which produce much fuller-bodied reds. Many Chiantis also benefit from the addition of a small amount of Cabernet Sauvignon.

Other well-known wines from Italy include Barbaresco, Bardolino, Trentino and Valpolicella. All these wines are produced from grapes that are local to the producers and good examples are worth looking out for.

White Wines

The most important white wine grapes are Garganega, Moscato, Malvasia, Trebbiano and Pinot Bianco. Garganega is the principal grape used in the production of Soave, although some cheaper blends add Trebbiano Toscano which sometimes dominates. It produces wines that are refreshing and soft, yet green-apple fresh.

Moscato (or Muscat) produces both dry and sweet wines and, most famously, is the grape used to make Asti Spumante. Sweet Muscats should be perfumed with grapes, honey,

apples and cigar tobacco flavours.

Malvasia is used in a range of wines, both dry and sweet. It is often blended with Trebbiano to make Frascati which when well done, adds a creamy nuttiness to it. It also produces some brilliantly rich dessert wines.

Trebbiano is a widely planted grape, especially the inferior Trebbiano Toscano which is easy to grow and has a very high yield. Trebbiano di Soave, from the Veneto, is much better and is used to form the backbone of some very good wines, including some Soaves.

Pinot Bianco is grown largely in Friuli where some very fine examples are produced. Full, honeyed and buttery, Pinot Bianco can be exceptional.

Other grapes and types of wine produced in Italy include Chardonnay, Pinot Grigio, Gewürztraminer, Orvieto, Riesling, Sauvignon Blanc, Sylvaner and Tokay.

Sparkling and Fortified Wines and Liqueurs

Italy also produces a number of sparkling wines, as well as some fine fortified wines and spirits. Prosecco, which can also be still, is a lovely fresh, light white, just off-dry wine which is perfect as an aperitif.

Asti Spumante has a very poor reputation – mainly based on snobbery. It is a delicious, refreshing, grapey drink and is very reliable. A bad example of this wine is hard to find. It should be drunk very young.

Moscato d'Asti is another sweet, fizzy wine with lots of fresh fruit flavours and is worth seeking out.

Marsala is a Sicilian wine with a delicious brown-sugar sweetness and a cutting acidity that makes it delightfully refreshing for a fortified dessert wine. Look out for Marsala Vergine and Sercial Madeira.

Vin Santo can be rather dull, but fine examples have a lot of rich, fruit flavours including apples, apricots and grape skins as well as chewy toffee, smoke and liquorice flavours.

Amaretto di Saronno is perhaps the best-known, almond-flavoured Italian liqueur. It is delicious with coffee and very useful in cooking.

Olive Oil

Italian cooking without olive oil is unimaginable. A staple ingredient in the Italian storecupboard, olive oil has been produced for centuries and has had dozens of uses, from body and hair ointment to making and fuelling terracotta lamps.

Olive trees were first introduced to Italy and France by the ancient Greeks who had been cultivating them since about 3000 BC. The plants thrive in the Mediterranean, although they grow all over the world wherever weather conditions are similar. They can thrive on poor, rocky soil where other crops cannot and require little attention.

The olive is a stone fruit and, depending on the variety, can be eaten either green or black. Olives are always green when unripe and turn black as they ripen, passing through varying colours from red, to purple and brown and shades in between. Some varieties are good for eating, like the Greek Kalamata or Spanish Manzanilla, but others are grown specifically for their oil. The quality of the oil depends on cultivation, harvesting, milling, climate and soil conditions as much as on the variety of the olive.

Once the olives are harvested, they are stored until the optimum moment for pressing – this can take from several hours to three days depending on conditions. Most manufacturers use modern machinery for pressing, but in some parts of the Mediterranean, traditional methods still prevail.

When ready, the olives are washed and crushed (it is the crushing that extracts the oil). Traditionally, this was done with large stone wheels. Today, stainless steel crushers are used to simultaneously crush, shear and rub the olives. They are then ground to a paste which is spread on to fibre mats, piled one on top of the other and placed in a large vertical press. A small amount of pressure is applied to extract the oil. This is the first cold pressing.

The quality of the oil is determined by its acidity level – the higher the acidity, the lower the quality. About 90 per cent of the oil extracted in the cold pressing is extra-virgin olive oil, which has an acidity of less than one per cent. The remaining oil and any oil subsequently pressed from the olives is processed further to produce other grades of olive oil.

Extra-Virgin Olive Oil Obtained from the first pressing of the olives, it is of the highest-quality and is the most expensive olive oil with the lowest acidity. It has a rich, deep flavour and colour and is best used raw as a dressing for plain grilled meat or fish, for use in salad dressings, or drizzled over soups. This type of oil, however, has a low smoke point which means that it will burn more readily than a more refined oil and is therefore less suitable for cooking.

Virgin Olive Oil Virgin olive oil is sometimes called pure olive oil, but is generally labelled as olive oil. This oil tends to be paler in colour with a less pronounced olive flavour. It has a higher acidity level and a higher smoke point so is better suited to cooking.

Also available are olive oils blended with vegetable or sunflower oils to produce so-called light oils. Do not be fooled into thinking that these oils contain less fat – the word light refers only to the flavour.

It is generally accepted that Italy produces some of the finest olive oils in the world. The main characteristics of an Italian oil are its deep green colour and its peppery aftertaste. The other main olive oil-producing countries are France, Greece and Spain. Each country produces oils with their own particular characteristics. Supermarkets now stock a wide variety of olive oils of varying quality, although price is usually a good indicator of quality. Own-brand oils will generally be blended from a variety of sources to produce a uniform result. It is worth looking out for single estate oils which, although more expensive, are of a superior quality and are much more interesting to cook with.

Vinegars

Vinegars have many culinary uses, not least in salad dressings. They are also useful in sauces to cut through richness or sweetness. Italians use a variety of vinegars, but perhaps the most popular in recent years has been balsamic vinegar.

Balsamic Vinegar This has been made in Modena for centuries, during which time the production method has hardly changed. Fresh grape juice is boiled in an open pot over a fire for at least a day, after which it is transferred to wooden vats for ageing. The ageing process can vary from a few months to a couple of years for the cheapest examples and up to 50 years for the most expensive. The older the vinegar, the darker and thicker it is. Again, price is a good indicator of age and quality.

Wine vinegar This is also popular in Italy. Although supermarkets sell red and white wine vinegars, as well as cider and sherry vinegars, it is worth seeking out good-quality, deeply coloured varieties, especially for use in sauces. These tend to have a more pronounced, concentrated wine flavour and a less sour, vinegary flavour.

White Bean Soup with Parmesan Croûtons

INGREDIENTS

Serves 4

3 thick slices of white bread, cut into
 1 cm/½ inch cubes
3 tbsp groundnut oil
2 tbsp Parmesan cheese, finely grated
1 tbsp light olive oil
1 large onion, peeled and
 finely chopped
50 g/2 oz unsmoked bacon lardons
 (or thick slices of bacon, diced)
1 tbsp fresh thyme leaves
2 x 400 g cannellini beans, drained
900 ml/1½ pints chicken stock
salt and freshly ground black pepper
1 tbsp prepared pesto sauce
50 g/2 oz piece of pepperoni
 sausage, diced
1 tbsp fresh lemon juice
1 tbsp fresh basil, roughly shredded

1 Preheat oven to 200°C/400°F/Gas Mark 6. Place the cubes of bread in a bowl and pour over the groundnut oil. Stir to coat the bread, then sprinkle over the Parmesan cheese. Place on a lightly oiled baking tray and bake in the preheated oven for 10 minutes, or until crisp and golden.

2 Heat the olive oil in a large saucepan and cook the onion for 4–5 minutes until softened. Add the bacon and thyme and cook for a further 3 minutes. Stir in the beans, stock and black pepper and simmer gently for 5 minutes.

3 Place half the bean mixture and liquid into a food processor and blend until smooth.

4 Return the purée to the saucepan. Stir in the pesto sauce, pepperoni sausage and lemon juice and season to taste with salt and pepper.

5 Return the soup to the heat and cook for a further 2–3 minutes, or until piping hot. Place some of the beans in each serving bowl and add a ladleful of soup. Garnish with shredded basil and serve immediately with the croûtons scattered over the top.

1

2

4

Rice Soup with Potato Sticks

INGREDIENTS

Serves 4

175 g/6 oz butter
1 tsp olive oil
1 large onion, peeled and
  finely chopped
4 slices Parma ham, chopped
100 g/3½ oz Arborio rice
1.1 litres/2 pints chicken stock
350 g/12 oz frozen peas
salt and freshly ground black pepper
1 medium egg
125 g/4 oz self-raising flour
175 g/6 oz mashed potato
1 tbsp milk
1 tbsp poppy seeds
1 tbsp Parmesan cheese, finely grated
1 tbsp freshly chopped parsley

1 Preheat oven to 190°C/375°F/Gas Mark 5. Heat 25 g/1 oz of the butter and the olive oil in a saucepan and cook the onion for 4–5 minutes until softened, then add the Parma ham and cook for about 1 minute. Stir in the rice, the stock and the peas. Season to taste with salt and pepper and simmer for 10–15 minutes, or until the rice is tender.

2 Beat the egg and 125 g/4 oz of the butter together until smooth, then beat in the flour, a pinch of salt and the potato. Work the ingredients together to form a soft, pliable dough, adding a little more flour if necessary.

3 Roll the dough out on a lightly floured surface into a rectangle 1 cm/½ inch thick and cut into 12 thin long sticks. Brush with milk and sprinkle on the poppy seeds. Place the sticks on a lightly oiled baking tray and bake in the preheated oven for 15 minutes, or until golden.

4 When the rice is cooked, stir the remaining butter and Parmesan cheese into the soup and sprinkle the chopped parsley over the top. Serve immediately with the warm potato sticks.

TASTY TIP

These potato sticks also make a delicious snack with drinks. Try sprinkling them with sesame seeds or grated cheese and allow to cool before serving.

1

2

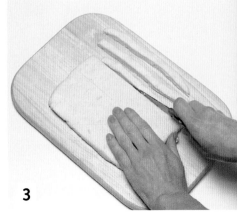

3

Rich Tomato Soup with Roasted Red Peppers

INGREDIENTS

Serves 4

2 tsp light olive oil

700 g/1½ lb red peppers, halved and deseeded

450 g/1 lb ripe plum tomatoes, halved

2 onions, unpeeled and quartered

4 garlic cloves, unpeeled

600 ml/1 pint chicken stock

salt and freshly ground black pepper

4 tbsp soured cream

1 tbsp freshly shredded basil

1 Preheat oven to 200°C/400°F/Gas Mark 6. Lightly oil a roasting tin with 1 teaspoon of the olive oil. Place the peppers and tomatoes cut side down in the roasting tin with the onion quarters and the garlic cloves. Spoon over the remaining oil.

2 Bake in the preheated oven for 30 minutes, or until the skins on the peppers have started to blacken and blister. Allow the vegetables to cool for about 10 minutes, then remove the skins, stalks and seeds from the peppers. Peel away the skins from the tomatoes and onions and squeeze out the garlic.

3 Place the cooked vegetables into a blender or food processor and blend until smooth. Add the stock and blend again to form a smooth purée. Pour the puréed soup through a sieve. If a smooth soup is preferred, then pour into a saucepan. Bring to the boil, simmer gently for 2–3 minutes, and season to taste with salt and pepper. Serve hot with a swirl of soured cream and a sprinkling of shredded basil on the top.

HELPFUL HINT

To help remove the skins of the peppers more easily, remove them from the oven and put immediately into a plastic bag or a bowl covered with clingfilm. Leave until cool enough to handle then skin carefully.

1

2

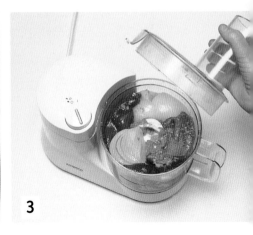

3

Bread & Tomato Soup

INGREDIENTS

Serves 4

900 g/2 lb very ripe tomatoes
4 tbsp olive oil
1 onion, peeled and finely chopped
1 tbsp freshly chopped basil
3 garlic cloves, peeled and crushed
¼ tsp hot chilli powder
salt and freshly ground black pepper
600 ml/1 pint chicken stock
175 g/6 oz stale white bread
50 g/2 oz cucumber, cut into
　small dice
4 whole basil leaves

1　Make a small cross in the base of each tomato, then place in a bowl and cover with boiling water. Allow to stand for 2 minutes, or until the skins have started to peel away, then drain, remove the skins and seeds and chop into large pieces.

2　Heat 3 tablespoons of the olive oil in a saucepan and gently cook the onion until softened. Add the skinned tomatoes, chopped basil, garlic and chilli powder and season to taste with salt and pepper. Pour in the stock, cover the saucepan, bring to the boil and simmer gently for 15–20 minutes.

3　Remove the crusts from the bread and break into small pieces. Remove the tomato mixture from the heat and stir in the bread. Cover and leave to stand for 10 minutes, or until the bread has blended with the tomatoes. Season to taste. Serve warm or cold with a swirl of olive oil on the top, garnished with a spoonful of chopped cucumber and basil leaves.

TASTY TIP

This soup is best made when fresh tomatoes are in season. If you want to make it at other times of the year, replace the fresh tomatoes with 2 x 400 g cans of peeled plum tomatoes – Italian, if possible. You may need to cook the soup for 5–10 minutes longer.

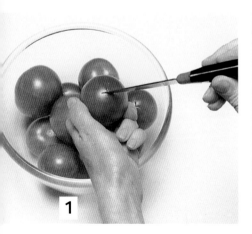
1

2

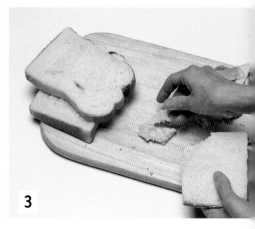
3

Rocket & Potato Soup with Garlic Croûtons

INGREDIENTS

Serves 4

700 g/1½ lb baby new potatoes
1.1 litres/2 pints chicken or
  vegetable stock
50 g/2 oz rocket leaves
125 g/4 oz thick white
  sliced bread
50 g/2 oz unsalted butter
1 tsp groundnut oil
2–4 garlic cloves, peeled and chopped
125 g/4 oz stale ciabatta bread, with
  the crusts removed
4 tbsp olive oil
salt and freshly ground black pepper
2 tbsp Parmesan cheese, finely grated

HELPFUL HINT
Rocket is now widely available in bags from most large supermarkets. If, however, you cannot get hold of it, replace it with an equal quantity of watercress or baby spinach leaves.

1 Place the potatoes in a large saucepan, cover with the stock and simmer gently for 10 minutes. Add the rocket leaves and simmer for a further 5–10 minutes, or until the potatoes are soft and the rocket has wilted.

2 Meanwhile, make the croûtons. Cut the thick white sliced bread into small cubes and reserve. Heat the butter and groundnut oil in a small frying pan and cook the garlic for 1 minute, stirring well. Remove the garlic. Add the bread cubes to the butter and oil mixture in the frying pan and sauté, stirring continuously, until they are golden brown. Drain the croûtons on absorbent kitchen paper and reserve.

3 Cut the ciabatta bread into small dice and stir into the soup. Cover the saucepan and leave to stand for 10 minutes, or until the bread has absorbed a lot of the liquid.

4 Stir in the olive oil, season to taste with salt and pepper and serve at once with a few of the garlic croûtons scattered over the top and a little grated Parmesan cheese.

Classic Minestrone

INGREDIENTS

Serves 6

25 g/1 oz butter
3 tbsp olive oil
3 rashers streaky bacon
1 large onion, peeled
1 garlic clove, peeled
1 celery stick, trimmed
2 carrots, peeled
400 g can chopped tomatoes
1.1 litre/2 pints chicken stock
175 g/6 oz green cabbage,
   finely shredded
50 g/2 oz French beans, trimmed
   and halved
3 tbsp frozen petits pois
50 g/2 oz spaghetti, broken into
   short pieces
salt and freshly ground black pepper
Parmesan cheese shavings,
   to garnish
crusty bread, to serve

1 Heat the butter and olive oil together in a large saucepan. Chop the bacon and add to the saucepan. Cook for 3–4 minutes, then remove with a slotted spoon and reserve.

2 Finely chop the onion, garlic, celery and carrots and add to the saucepan, one ingredient at a time, stirring well after each addition. Cover and cook gently for 8–10 minutes, until the vegetables are softened.

3 Add the chopped tomatoes, with their juice and the stock, bring to the boil then cover the saucepan with a lid, reduce the heat and simmer gently for about 20 minutes.

4 Stir in the cabbage, beans, peas and spaghetti pieces. Cover and simmer for a further 20 minutes, or until all the ingredients are tender. Season to taste with salt and pepper.

5 Return the cooked bacon to the saucepan and bring the soup to the boil. Serve the soup immediately with Parmesan cheese shavings sprinkled on the top and plenty of crusty bread to accompany it.

TASTY TIP

For a vegetarian version, omit the bacon and use vegetable stock and a vegetarian cheese.

Cream of Pumpkin Soup

INGREDIENTS

Serves 4

900 g/2 lb pumpkin flesh (after
   peeling and discarding the seeds)
4 tbsp olive oil
1 large onion, peeled
1 leek, trimmed
1 carrot, peeled
2 celery sticks
4 garlic cloves, peeled and crushed
1.7 litres/3 pints water
salt and freshly ground black pepper
¼ tsp freshly grated nutmeg
150 ml/¼ pint single cream
¼ tsp cayenne pepper
warm herby bread, to serve

1 Cut the skinned and de-seeded pumpkin flesh into 2.5 cm/1 inch cubes. Heat the olive oil in a large saucepan and cook the pumpkin for 2–3 minutes, coating it completely with oil. Chop the onion and leek finely and cut the carrot and celery into small dice.

2 Add the vegetables to the saucepan with the garlic and cook, stirring for 5 minutes, or until they have begun to soften. Cover the vegetables with the water and bring to the boil. Season with plenty of salt and pepper and the nutmeg, cover and simmer for 15–20 minutes, or until all of the vegetables are tender.

3 When the vegetables are tender, remove from the heat, cool slightly then pour into a food processor or blender. Liquidise to form a smooth purée, then pass through a sieve into a clean saucepan.

4 Adjust the seasoning to taste and add all but 2 tablespoons of the cream and enough water to obtain the correct consistency. Bring the soup to boiling point, add the cayenne pepper and serve immediately swirled with cream and warm herby bread.

TASTY TIP

If you cannot find pumpkin, try replacing it with squash. Butternut, acorn or turban squash would all make suitable substitutes. Avoid spaghetti squash which is not firm-fleshed when cooked.

Lettuce Soup

INGREDIENTS

Serves 4

2 iceberg lettuces, quartered with
   hard core removed
1 tbsp olive oil
50 g/2 oz butter
125 g/4 oz spring onions, trimmed
   and chopped
1 tbsp freshly chopped parsley
1 tbsp plain flour
600 ml/1 pint chicken stock
salt and freshly ground black pepper
150 ml/¼ pint single cream
¼ tsp cayenne pepper, to taste
thick slices of stale ciabatta bread
sprigs of parsley, to garnish

1 Bring a large saucepan of water to the boil and blanch the lettuce leaves for 3 minutes. Drain and dry thoroughly on absorbent kitchen paper. Then shred with a sharp knife.

2 Heat the oil and butter in a clean saucepan and add the lettuce, spring onions and parsley and cook together for 3–4 minutes, or until very soft.

3 Stir in the flour and cook for 1 minute, then gradually pour in the stock, stirring throughout. Bring to the boil and season to taste with salt and pepper. Reduce the heat, cover and simmer gently for 10–15 minutes, or until soft.

4 Allow the soup to cool slightly, then either sieve or purée in a blender. Alternatively, leave the soup chunky. Stir in the cream, add more seasoning, to taste, if liked, then add the cayenne pepper.

5 Arrange the slices of ciabatta bread in a large soup dish or in individual bowls and pour the soup over the bread. Garnish with sprigs of parsley and serve immediately.

HELPFUL HINT

Do not prepare the lettuce too far in advance. Iceberg lettuce has a tendency to discolour when sliced, which may in turn discolour the soup.

2

3

4

Antipasti with Focaccia

INGREDIENTS

Serves 4

3 fresh figs, quartered

125 g/4 oz green beans, cooked
  and halved

1 small head of radicchio, rinsed
  and shredded

125 g/4 oz large prawns, peeled
  and cooked

125 can sardines, drained

25 g/1 oz pitted black olives

25 g/1 oz stuffed green olives

125 g/4 oz mozzarella cheese, sliced

50 g/2 oz Italian salami sausage,
  thinly sliced

3 tbsp olive oil

275 g/10 oz strong white flour

pinch of sugar

3 tsp easy-blend quick-acting yeast or
  15 g/¹⁄₂ oz fresh yeast

175 g/6 oz fine semolina

1 tsp salt

300 ml/¹⁄₂ pint warm water

a little extra olive oil for brushing

1 tbsp coarse salt crystals

1 Preheat oven to 220°C/425°F/Gas Mark 7, 15 minutes before baking. Arrange the fresh fruit, vegetables, prawns, sardines, olives, cheese and meat on a large serving platter. Drizzle over 1 tablespoon of the olive oil, then cover and chill in the refrigerator while making the bread.

2 Sift the flour, sugar, semolina and salt into a large mixing bowl then sprinkle in the dried yeast. Make a well in the centre and add the remaining 2 tablespoons of olive oil. Add the warm water, a little at a time, and mix together until a smooth, pliable dough is formed. If using fresh yeast, cream the yeast with the sugar, then gradually beat in half the warm water. Leave in a warm place until frothy then proceed as for dried yeast.

3 Place on to a lightly floured board and knead until smooth and elastic. Place the dough in a lightly greased bowl, cover and leave in a warm place for 45 minutes.

4 Knead again and flatten the dough into a large, flat oval shape about 1 cm/¹⁄₂ inch thick. Place on a lightly oiled baking tray. Prick the surface with the end of a wooden spoon and brush with olive oil. Sprinkle on the coarse salt and bake in the preheated oven for 25 minutes, or until golden. Serve the bread with the prepared platter of food.

1

2

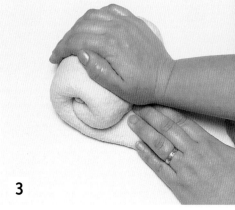

3

Mozzarella Frittata
with Tomato & Basil Salad

INGREDIENTS

Serves 6

For the salad:
6 ripe but firm tomatoes
2 tbsp fresh basil leaves
2 tbsp olive oil
1 tbsp fresh lemon juice
1 tsp caster sugar
freshly ground black pepper

For the frittata:
7 medium eggs, beaten
salt
300 g/11 oz mozzarella cheese
2 spring onions, trimmed and
  finely chopped
2 tbsp olive oil
warm crusty bread, to serve

HELPFUL HINT
Fresh mozzarella is sold in packets and is usually surrounded by a light brine. After grating the cheese, firmly press between layers of absorbent kitchen paper to remove any excess water which might leak out during cooking.

1 To make the tomato and basil salad, slice the tomatoes very thinly, tear up the basil leaves and sprinkle over. Make the dressing by whisking the olive oil, lemon juice and sugar together well. Season with black pepper before drizzling the dressing over the salad.

2 To make the frittata, preheat the grill to a high heat, just before beginning to cook. Place the eggs in a large bowl with plenty of salt and whisk. Grate the mozzarella and stir into the egg with the finely chopped spring onions.

3 Heat the oil in a large, non-stick frying pan and pour in the egg mixture, stirring with a wooden spoon to spread the ingredients evenly over the pan.

4 Cook for 5–8 minutes, until the frittata is golden brown and firm on the underside. Place the whole pan under the preheated grill and cook for about 4–5 minutes, or until the top is golden brown. Slide the frittata on to a serving plate, cut into 6 large wedges and serve immediately with the tomato and basil salad and plenty of warm crusty bread.

2

3

4

Fried Whitebait with Rocket Salad

INGREDIENTS

Serves 4

450 g/1 lb whitebait, fresh or frozen
oil, for frying
85 g/3 oz plain flour
½ tsp of cayenne pepper
salt and freshly ground black pepper

For the salad:

125 g/4 oz rocket leaves
125 g/4 oz cherry tomatoes, halved
75 g/3 oz cucumber, cut into dice
3 tbsp olive oil
1 tbsp fresh lemon juice
½ tsp Dijon mustard
½ tsp caster sugar

1 If the whitebait are frozen, thaw completely, then wipe dry with absorbent kitchen paper.

2 Start to heat the oil in a deep-fat fryer. Arrange the fish in a large, shallow dish and toss well in the flour, cayenne pepper and salt and pepper.

3 Deep fry the fish in batches for 2–3 minutes, or until crisp and golden. Keep the cooked fish warm while deep frying the remaining fish.

4 Meanwhile, to make the salad, arrange the rocket leaves, cherry tomatoes and cucumber on individual serving dishes. Whisk the olive oil and the remaining ingredients together and season lightly. Drizzle the dressing over the salad and serve with the whitebait.

TASTY TIP

Why not try a different salad? Mix together some cleaned baby spinach, cooled, cooked petits pois and chopped spring onions, then pour over 2 tablespoons of garlic olive oil. If serving with a chicken dish, top the salad with some feta cheese.

1

2

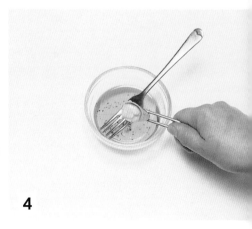

4

Bruschetta with Pecorino, Garlic & Tomatoes

INGREDIENTS

Serves 4

6 ripe but firm tomatoes

125 g/4 oz pecorino cheese,
  finely grated

1 tbsp oregano leaves

salt and freshly ground black pepper

3 tbsp olive oil

3 garlic cloves, peeled

8 slices of flat Italian bread, such
  as focaccia

50 g/2 oz mozzarella cheese

marinated black olives, to serve

1 Preheat grill and line the grill rack with tinfoil just before cooking. Make a small cross in the top of the tomatoes, then place in a small bowl and cover with boiling water. Leave to stand for 2 minutes, then drain and remove the skins. Cut into quarters, remove the seeds, and chop the flesh into small dice.

2 Mix the tomato flesh with the pecorino cheese and 2 teaspoons of the fresh oregano and season to taste with salt and pepper. Add 1 tablespoon of the olive oil and mix thoroughly.

3 Crush the garlic and spread evenly over the slices of bread. Heat 2 tablespoons of the olive oil in a large frying pan and sauté the bread slices until they are crisp and golden.

4 Place the fried bread on a lightly oiled baking tray and spoon on the tomato and cheese topping. Place a little mozzarella on top and place under the preheated grill for 3–4 minutes, until golden and bubbling. Garnish with the remaining oregano, then arrange the bruschettas on a serving plate and serve immediately with the olives.

TASTY TIP

Bitter leaves are excellent with these bruschettas because they help to offset the richness of the cheese and tomato topping. Try a mixture of frisée, radicchio and rocket. If these are unavailable, use a bag of mixed salad leaves.

1

2

3

Crostini with Chicken Livers

INGREDIENTS

Serves 4

2 tbsp olive oil
2 tbsp butter
1 shallot, peeled and finely chopped
1 garlic clove, peeled and crushed
150 g/5 oz chicken livers
1 tbsp plain flour
2 tbsp dry white wine
1 tbsp brandy
50 g/2 oz mushrooms, sliced
salt and freshly ground black pepper
4 slices of ciabatta or similar bread

To garnish:

fresh sage leaves
lemon wedges

TASTY TIP

If you prefer a lower fat alternative to the fried bread in this recipe, omit 1 tablespoon of the butter and brush the bread slices with the remaining 1 tablespoon of oil. Bake in a preheated oven 180°C/350°F/Gas Mark 4 for about 20 minutes, or until golden and crisp then serve as above.

1 Heat 1 tablespoon of the olive oil and 1 tablespoon of the butter in a frying pan, add the shallot and garlic and cook gently for 2–3 minutes.

2 Trim and wash the chicken livers thoroughly and pat dry on absorbent kitchen paper as much as possible. Cut into slices, then toss in the flour. Add the livers to the frying pan with the shallot and garlic and continue to fry for a further 2 minutes, stirring continuously.

3 Pour in the white wine and brandy and bring to the boil. Boil rapidly for 1–2 minutes to allow the alcohol to evaporate, then stir in the sliced mushrooms and cook gently for about 5 minutes, or until the chicken livers are cooked, but just a little pink inside. Season to taste with salt and pepper.

4 Fry the slices of ciabatta or similar-style bread in the remaining oil and butter, then place on individual serving dishes. Spoon over the liver mixture and garnish with a few sage leaves and lemon wedges. Serve immediately.

2

3

3

Italian Baked Tomatoes with Curly Endive & Radicchio

INGREDIENTS

Serves 4

1 tsp olive oil
4 beef tomatoes
salt
50 g/2 oz fresh white breadcrumbs
1 tbsp freshly snipped chives
1 tbsp freshly chopped parsley
125 g/4 oz button mushrooms,
  finely chopped
salt and freshly ground black pepper
25 g/1 oz fresh Parmesan
  cheese, grated

For the salad:

½ curly endive lettuce
½ small piece of radicchio
2 tbsp olive oil
1 tsp balsamic vinegar
salt and freshly ground black pepper

TASTY TIP

As an alternative, try stirring in either 2 tablespoons of tapenade or ready-made pesto into the stuffing mixture. Alternatively, replace the chives with freshly chopped basil.

1 Preheat oven to 190°C/375°F/Gas Mark 5. Lightly oil a baking tray with the teaspoon of oil. Slice the tops off the tomatoes and remove all the tomato flesh and sieve into a large bowl. Sprinkle a little salt inside the tomato shells and then place them upside down on a plate while the filling is prepared.

2 Mix the sieved tomato with the breadcrumbs, fresh herbs and mushrooms and season well with salt and pepper. Place the tomato shells on the prepared baking tray and fill with the tomato and mushroom mixture. Sprinkle the cheese on the top and bake in the preheated oven for 15–20 minutes, until golden brown.

3 Meanwhile, prepare the salad. Arrange the endive and radicchio on individual serving plates and mix the remaining ingredients together in a small bowl to make the dressing. Season to taste.

4 When the tomatoes are cooked, allow to rest for 5 minutes, then place on the prepared plates and drizzle over a little dressing. Serve warm.

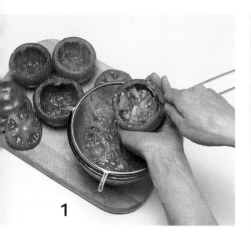

1

2

2

Spaghettini with Lemon Pesto & Cheese & Herb Bread

INGREDIENTS

Serves 4

1 small onion, peeled and grated

2 tsp freshly chopped oregano

1 tbsp freshly chopped parsley

75 g/3 oz butter

125 g/4 oz pecorino cheese, grated

8 slices of Italian flat bread

275 g/10 oz dried spaghettini

4 tbsp olive oil

1 large bunch of basil, approximately
  30 g/1 oz

75 g/3 oz pine nuts

1 garlic clove, peeled and crushed

75 g/3 oz Parmesan cheese, grated

finely grated rind and juice of
  2 lemons

salt and freshly ground black pepper

4 tsp butter

TASTY TIP

It is important to use a good-quality, full-flavoured olive oil for this recipe. Look for an extra-virgin or cold-pressed oil and buy the best you can afford.

1 Preheat oven to 200°C/400°F/Gas Mark 6, 15 minutes before baking. Mix together the onion, oregano, parsley, butter and cheese. Spread the bread with the cheese mixture, place on a lightly oiled baking tray and cover with tinfoil. Bake in the preheated oven for 10–15 minutes, then keep warm.

2 Add the spaghettini with 1 tablespoon of olive oil to a large saucepan of fast-boiling, lightly salted water and cook for 3–4 minutes, or until 'al dente'. Drain, reserving 2 tablespoons of the cooking liquor.

3 Blend the basil, pine nuts, garlic, Parmesan cheese, lemon rind and juice and remaining olive oil in a food processor or blender until a purée is formed. Season to taste with salt and pepper, then place in a saucepan.

4 Heat the lemon pesto very gently until piping hot, then stir in the pasta together with the reserved cooking liquor. Add the butter and mix well together.

5 Add plenty of black pepper to the pasta and serve immediately with the warm cheese and herb bread.

1

3

4

Mussels with Creamy Garlic & Saffron Sauce

INGREDIENTS

Serves 4

700 g/1½ lb fresh live mussels
300 ml/½ pint good-quality dry
  white wine
1 tbsp olive oil
1 shallot, peeled and finely chopped
2 garlic cloves, peeled and crushed
1 tbsp freshly chopped oregano
2 saffron strands
150 ml/¼ pint single cream
salt and freshly ground black pepper
fresh crusty bread, to serve

HELPFUL HINT

Mussels are now farmed and are available most of the year. However, always try to buy mussels the day you intend to eat them. Place them in a bowl of cold water in the refrigerator as soon as possible, changing the water at least every 2 hours. If live mussels are unavailable, use prepacked, cooked mussels.

1 Clean the mussels thoroughly in plenty of cold water and remove any beards and barnacles from the shells. Discard any mussels that are open or damaged. Place in a large bowl and cover with cold water and leave in the refrigerator until required, if prepared earlier.

2 Pour the wine into a large saucepan and bring to the boil. Tip the mussels into the pan, cover and cook, shaking the saucepan periodically for 6–8 minutes, or until the mussels have opened completely.

3 Discard any mussels with closed shells, then using a slotted spoon, carefully remove the remaining open mussels from the saucepan and keep them warm. Reserve the cooking liquor.

4 Heat the olive oil in a small frying pan and cook the shallot and garlic gently for 2–3 minutes, until softened. Add the reserved cooking liquid and chopped oregano and cook for a further 3–4 minutes. Stir in the saffron and the cream and heat through gently. Season to taste with salt and pepper. Place a few mussels in individual serving bowls and spoon over the saffron sauce. Serve immediately with plenty of fresh crusty bread.

Peperonata (Braised Mixed Peppers)

INGREDIENTS

Serves 4

2 green peppers
1 red pepper
1 yellow pepper
1 orange pepper
1 onion, peeled
2 garlic cloves, peeled
2 tbsp olive oil
4 very ripe tomatoes
1 tbsp freshly chopped oregano
salt and freshly ground black pepper
150 ml/¼ pint light chicken or
   vegetable stock
sprigs of fresh oregano, to garnish
focaccia (see recipe p. 32) or flat
   bread, to serve

1 Remove the seeds from the peppers and cut into thin strips. Slice the onion into rings and chop the garlic cloves finely.

2 Heat the olive oil in a frying pan and fry the peppers, onions and garlic for 5–10 minutes, or until soft and lightly coloured. Stir continuously.

3 Make a cross on the top of the tomatoes then place in a bowl and cover with boiling water. Allow to stand for about 2 minutes. Drain, then remove the skins and seeds and chop the tomato flesh into cubes.

4 Add the tomatoes and oregano to the peppers and onion and season to taste with salt and pepper. Cover the pan and bring to the boil. Simmer gently for about 30 minutes, or until tender, adding the chicken or vegetable stock halfway through the cooking time.

5 Garnish with sprigs of oregano and serve hot with plenty of freshly baked focaccia bread or alternatively lightly toast slices of flat bread and pile a spoonful of peperonata on to each plate.

TASTY TIP

Serve the peperonata cold as part of an antipasti platter. Some good accompaniments would be marinated olives, sun-dried or semi-dried marinated tomatoes, sliced salamis and other cold meats, and plenty of Italian bread.

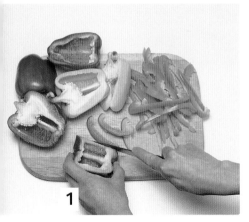

Wild Garlic Mushrooms with Pizza Breadsticks

INGREDIENTS

Serves 6

For the breadsticks:

7 g/¼ oz dried yeast
250 ml/8 fl oz warm water
400 g/14 oz strong, plain flour
2 tbsp olive oil
1 tsp salt

For the mushrooms:

9 tbsp olive oil
4 garlic cloves, peeled and crushed
450 g/1 lb mixed wild mushrooms, wiped and dried
salt and freshly ground black pepper
1 tbsp freshly chopped parsley
1 tbsp freshly chopped basil
1 tsp fresh oregano leaves
juice of 1 lemon

HELPFUL HINT

Never clean mushrooms under running water. Mushrooms absorb liquid very easily and then release it again during cooking, making the dish watery.

1 Preheat oven to 240°C/475°F/Gas Mark 9, 15 minutes before baking. Place the dried yeast in the warm water for 10 minutes. Place the flour in a large bowl and gradually blend in the olive oil, salt and the dissolved yeast.

2 Knead on a lightly floured surface to form a smooth and pliable dough. Cover with clingfilm and leave in a warm place for 15 minutes to allow the dough to rise, then roll out again and cut into sticks of equal length. Cover and leave to rise again for 10 minutes. Brush with the olive oil, sprinkle with salt and bake in the preheated oven for 10 minutes.

3 Pour 3 tablespoons of the oil into a frying pan and add the crushed garlic. Cook over a very low heat, stirring well for 3–4 minutes to flavour the oil.

4 Cut the wild mushrooms into bite-sized slices if very large, then add to the pan. Season well with salt and pepper and cook very gently for 6–8 minutes, or until tender.

5 Whisk the fresh herbs, the remaining olive oil and lemon juice together. Pour over the mushrooms and heat through. Season to taste and place on individual serving dishes. Serve with the pizza breadsticks.

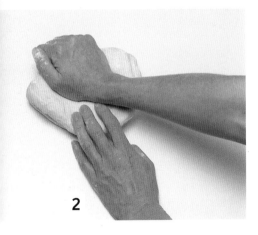

2

2

4

Hot Tiger Prawns with Parma Ham

INGREDIENTS

Serves 4

½ cucumber, peeled if preferred
4 ripe tomatoes
12 raw tiger prawns
6 tbsp olive oil
4 garlic cloves, peeled and crushed
4 tbsp freshly chopped parsley
salt and freshly ground black pepper
6 slices of Parma ham, cut in half
4 slices flat Italian bread
4 tbsp dry white wine

HELPFUL HINT

The black intestinal vein needs to be removed from raw prawns because it can cause a bitter flavour. Remove the shell, then using a small, sharp knife, make a cut along the centre back of the prawn and open out the flesh. Using the tip of the knife, remove the thread that lies along the length of the prawn and discard.

1 Preheat oven to 180°C/350°F/Gas Mark 4. Slice the cucumber and tomatoes thinly, then arrange on 4 large plates and reserve. Peel the prawns, leaving the tail shell intact and remove the thin black vein running down the back.

2 Whisk together 4 tablespoons of the olive oil, garlic and chopped parsley in a small bowl and season to taste with plenty of salt and pepper. Add the prawns to the mixture and stir until they are well coated. Remove the prawns, then wrap each one in a piece of Parma ham and secure with a cocktail stick.

3 Place the prepared prawns on a lightly oiled baking sheet or dish with the slices of bread and cook in the preheated oven for 5 minutes.

4 Remove the prawns from the oven and spoon the wine over the prawns and bread. Return to the oven and cook for a further 10 minutes until piping hot.

5 Carefully remove the cocktail sticks and arrange 3 prawn rolls on each slice of bread. Place on top of the sliced cucumber and tomatoes and serve immediately.

2

2

4

Mozzarella Parcels with Cranberry Relish

INGREDIENTS

Serves 6

125 g/4 oz mozzarella cheese
8 slices of thin white bread
2 medium eggs, beaten
salt and freshly ground black pepper
300 ml/½ pint olive oil

For the relish:

125 g/4 oz cranberries
2 tbsp fresh orange juice
grated rind of 1 small orange
50 g/2 oz soft light brown sugar
1 tbsp port

HELPFUL HINT

Frying in oil that is not hot enough causes food to absorb more oil than it would if fried at the correct temperature. To test the temperature of the oil without a thermometer, drop a cube of bread into the frying pan. If the bread browns in 30 seconds the oil is at the right temperature.

1 Slice the mozzarella thinly, remove the crusts from the bread and make sandwiches with the bread and cheese. Cut into 5 cm/2 inch squares and squash them quite flat. Season the eggs with salt and pepper, then soak the bread in the seasoned egg for 1 minute on each side until well coated.

2 Heat the oil to 190°C/ 375°F and deep-fry the bread squares for 1–2 minutes, or until they are crisp and golden brown. Drain on absorbent kitchen paper and keep warm while the cranberry relish is prepared.

3 Place the cranberries, orange juice, rind, sugar and port into a small saucepan and add 5 tablespoons of water. Bring to the boil, then simmer for 10 minutes, or until the cranberries have 'popped'. Sweeten with a little more sugar if necessary.

4 Arrange the mozzarella parcels on individual serving plates. Serve with a little of the cranberry relish.

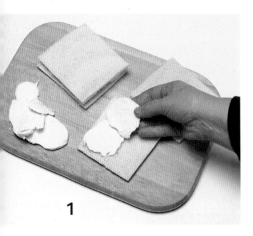
1

1

3

Pea & Prawn Risotto

INGREDIENTS

Serves 6

450 g/1 lb whole raw prawns

125 g/4 oz butter

1 red onion, peeled and chopped

4 garlic cloves, peeled and
finely chopped

225 g/8 oz Arborio rice

150 ml/¼ pint dry white wine

1.1 litres/2 pints vegetable or
fish stock

375 g/13 oz frozen peas

4 tbsp freshly chopped mint

salt and freshly ground black pepper

TASTY TIP

Frying the prawn shells and heads before cooking the dish adds a great deal of flavour to the rice. Alternatively, the shells and heads could be added to the stock and simmered for 10 minutes. Strain the stock, pressing the shells and heads well to extract the maximum flavour.

1. Peel the prawns and reserve the heads and shells. Remove the black vein from the back of each prawn, then wash and dry on absorbent kitchen paper. Melt half the butter in a large frying pan, add the prawns' heads and shells and fry, stirring occasionally for 3–4 minutes, or until golden. Strain the butter, discard the heads and shells and return the butter to the pan.

2. Add a further 25 g/1 oz of butter to the pan and fry the onion and garlic for 5 minutes until softened, but not coloured. Add the rice and stir the grains in the butter for 1 minute, until they are coated thoroughly. Add the white wine and boil rapidly until the wine is reduced by half.

3. Bring the stock to a gentle simmer, and add to the rice, a ladleful at a time. Stir constantly, adding the stock as it is absorbed, until the rice is creamy, but still has a bite in the centre.

4. Melt the remaining butter and stir-fry the prawns for 3–4 minutes. Stir into the rice, along with all the pan juices and the peas. Add the chopped mint and season to taste with salt and pepper. Cover the pan and leave the prawns to infuse for 5 minutes before serving.

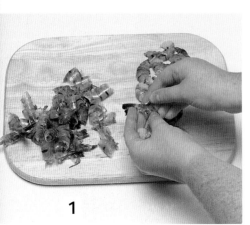

1

1

2

Stuffed Squid with Romesco Sauce

INGREDIENTS

Serves 4

8 small squid, about 350 g/12 oz
5 tbsp olive oil
50 g/2 oz pancetta, diced
1 onion, peeled and chopped
3 garlic cloves, peeled and
  finely chopped
2 tsp freshly chopped thyme
50 g/2 oz sun-dried tomatoes in oil
  drained, and chopped
75 g/3 oz fresh white breadcrumbs
2 tbsp freshly chopped basil
juice of ½ lime
salt and freshly ground black pepper
2 vine-ripened tomatoes, peeled and
  finely chopped
pinch of dried chilli flakes
1 tsp dried oregano
1 large red pepper, skinned
  and chopped
assorted salad leaves, to serve

1 Preheat oven to 230°C/450°F/Gas Mark 8, 15 minutes before cooking. Clean the squid if necessary, rinse lightly, pat dry with absorbent kitchen paper and finely chop the tentacles.

2 Heat 2 tablespoons of the olive oil in a large non-stick frying pan and fry the pancetta for 5 minutes, or until crisp. Remove the pancetta and reserve. Add the tentacles, onion, 2 garlic cloves, thyme and sun-dried tomatoes to the oil remaining in the pan and cook gently for 5 minutes, or until softened.

3 Remove the pan from the heat and stir in the diced pancetta. Blend in a food processor if a smoother stuffing is preferred, then stir in the breadcrumbs, basil and lime juice. Season to taste with salt and pepper and reserve. Spoon the stuffing into the cavity of the squid and secure the tops with cocktail sticks.

4 Place the squid in a large roasting tin, and sprinkle over 2 tablespoons each of oil and water. Place in the preheated oven and cook or 20 minutes.

5 Heat the remaining oil in a saucepan and cook the remaining garlic for 3 minutes. Add the tomatoes, chilli flakes and oregano and simmer gently for 15 minutes before stirring in the red pepper. Cook gently for a further 5 minutes. Blend in a food processor to make a smooth sauce and season to taste. Pour the sauce over the squid and serve immediately with some assorted salad leaves.

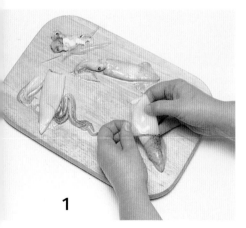

1

2

3

Scallops & Monkfish Kebabs with Fennel Sauce

INGREDIENTS

Serves 4

700 g/1½ lb monkfish tail
8 large fresh scallops
2 tbsp olive oil
1 garlic clove, peeled and crushed
freshly ground black pepper
1 fennel bulb, trimmed and
  thinly sliced
assorted salad leaves, to serve

For the sauce:

2 tbsp fennel seeds
pinch of chilli flakes
4 tbsp olive oil
2 tsp lemon juice
salt and freshly ground black pepper

1 Place the monkfish on a chopping board and remove the skin and the bone that runs down the centre of the tail and discard. Lightly rinse and pat dry with absorbent kitchen paper. Cut the 2 fillets into 12 equal-sized pieces and place in a shallow bowl.

2 Remove the scallops from their shells, if necessary, and clean thoroughly discarding the black vein. Rinse lightly and pat dry with absorbent kitchen paper. Put in the bowl with the fish.

3 Blend the 2 tablespoons of olive oil, the crushed garlic and a pinch of black pepper in a small bowl, then pour the mixture over the monkfish and scallops, making sure they are well coated. Cover lightly and leave to marinate in the refrigerator for at least 30 minutes, or longer if time permits. Spoon over the marinade occasionally.

4 Lightly crush the fennel seeds and chilli flakes in a pestle and mortar. Stir in the 4 tablespoons of olive oil and lemon juice and season to taste with salt and pepper. Cover and leave to infuse for 20 minutes.

5 Drain the monkfish and scallops, reserving the marinade and thread on to 4 skewers.

6 Spray a griddle pan with a fine spray of oil, then heat until almost smoking and cook the kebabs for 5–6 minutes, turning halfway through and brushing with the marinade throughout.

7 Brush the fennel slices with the fennel sauce and cook on the griddle for 1 minute on each side. Serve the fennel slices, topped with the kebabs and drizzled with the fennel sauce. Serve with a few assorted salad leaves.

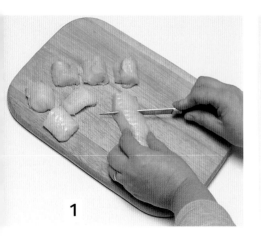

1

3

4

Red Pesto & Clam Spaghetti

INGREDIENTS

Serves 4

For the red pesto:

2 garlic cloves, peeled and
   finely chopped
50 g/2 oz pine nuts
25 g/1 oz fresh basil leaves
4 sun-dried tomatoes in oil, drained
4 tbsp olive oil
4 tbsp Parmesan cheese, grated
salt and freshly ground black pepper

For the clam sauce:

450 g/1 lb live clams, in
   their shells
1 tbsp olive oil
2 garlic cloves, peeled and crushed
1 small onion, peeled and chopped
5 tbsp medium dry white wine
150 ml/¼ pint fish or chicken stock
275 g/10 oz spaghetti

TASTY TIP

This dish looks particularly attractive with the clams left in their shells. If you prefer, you could remove the meat from the shells at the end of step 3, leaving a few in for garnishing.

1 To make the red pesto, place the garlic, pine nuts, basil leaves, sun-dried tomatoes and olive oil in a food processor and blend in short, sharp bursts until smooth. Scrape into a bowl, then stir in the Parmesan cheese and season to taste with salt and pepper. Cover and leave in the refrigerator until required.

2 Scrub the clams with a soft brush and remove any beards from the shells, discard any shells that are open or damaged. Wash in plenty of cold water then leave in a bowl covered with cold water in the refrigerator until required. Change the water frequently.

3 Heat the olive oil in a large saucepan and gently fry the garlic and onion for 5 minutes until softened, but not coloured. Add the wine and stock and bring to the boil. Add the clams, cover and cook for 3–4 minutes, or until the clams have opened.

4 Discard any clams that have not opened and stir in the red pesto sauce. Bring a large saucepan of lightly salted water to the boil and cook the spaghetti for 5–7 minutes, or until 'al dente'. Drain and return to the saucepan. Add the sauce to the spaghetti, mix well, then spoon into a serving dish and serve immediately.

1

3   4

Sardines in Vine Leaves

INGREDIENTS

Serves 4

8–16 vine leaves in brine, drained
2 spring onions
6 tbsp olive oil
2 tbsp lime juice
2 tbsp freshly chopped oregano
1 tsp mustard powder
salt and freshly ground black pepper
8 sardines, cleaned
8 bay leaves
8 sprigs of fresh dill

To garnish:
lime wedges
sprigs of fresh dill

To serve:
olive salad
crusty bread

HELPFUL HINT

To clean sardines, insert a knife and make a cut along the belly. Remove the insides and discard. Wash the fish well. Remove the scales by gently rubbing your thumb along the fish from tail to head. Sardines have very delicate skin, so rub gently.

1 Preheat the grill and line the grill rack with tinfoil just before cooking. Cut 8 pieces of string about 25.5 cm/10 inches long, and leave to soak in cold water for about 10 minutes. Cover the vine leaves in almost boiling water. Leave for 20 minutes, then drain and rinse thoroughly. Pat the vine leaves dry with absorbent kitchen paper.

2 Trim the spring onions and finely chop, then place into a small bowl. With a balloon whisk beat in the olive oil, lime juice, oregano, mustard powder and season to taste with salt and pepper. Cover with clingfilm and leave in the refrigerator, until required. Stir the mixture before using.

3 Prepare the sardines by making 2 slashes on both sides of each fish and brush with a little of the lime juice mixture. Place a bay leaf and a dill sprig inside each sardine cavity and wrap with 1–2 vine leaves, depending on size. Brush with the lime mixture and tie the vine leaves in place with string.

4 Grill the fish for 4–5 minutes on each side under a medium heat, brushing with a little more of the lime mixture if necessary. Leave the fish to rest, unwrap and discard the vine leaves. Garnish with lime wedges and sprigs of fresh dill and serve with the remaining lime mixture, olive salad and crusty bread.

1

3

3

Parmesan & Garlic Lobster

INGREDIENTS

Serves 2

1 large cooked lobster
25 g/1 oz unsalted butter
4 garlic cloves, peeled and crushed
1 tbsp plain flour
300 ml/½ pint milk
125 g/4 oz Parmesan cheese, grated
sea salt and freshly ground
  black pepper
assorted salad leaves, to serve

FOOD FACT

Nowadays we consider lobster to be a luxury, however, up until the end of 19th century lobster was so plentiful that it was used as fish bait.

HELPFUL HINT

This impressive-looking dish makes a wonderful starter for two. Make the sauce in advance and cover the surface with a layer of clingfilm. Refrigerate until ready to use.

1 Preheat oven to 180°C/350°F/Gas Mark 4, 10 minutes before cooking. Halve the lobster and crack the claws. Remove the gills, green sac behind the head and the black vein running down the body. Place the 2 lobster halves in a shallow ovenproof dish.

2 Melt the butter in a small saucepan and gently cook the garlic for 3 minutes, until softened. Add the flour and stir over a medium heat for 1 minute. Draw the saucepan off the heat then gradually stir in the milk, stirring until the sauce thickens. Return to the heat and cook for 2 minutes, stirring throughout until smooth and thickened. Stir in half the cheese and continue to cook for 1 minute, then season to taste with salt and pepper.

3 Pour the cheese sauce over the lobster halves and sprinkle with the remaining Parmesan cheese. Bake in the preheated oven for 20 minutes, or until heated through and the cheese sauce is golden brown. Serve with assorted salad leaves.

1

2

3

Roasted Cod with Saffron Aïoli

INGREDIENTS

Serves 4

For the saffron aïoli:

2 garlic cloves, peeled

¼ tsp saffron strands

sea salt, to taste

1 medium egg yolk

200 ml/7 fl oz extra-virgin
  olive oil

2 tbsp lemon juice

For the marinade:

2 tbsp olive oil

4 garlic cloves, peeled and
  finely chopped

1 red onion, peeled and
  finely chopped

1 tbsp freshly chopped rosemary

2 tbsp freshly chopped thyme

4–6 sprigs of fresh rosemary

1 lemon, sliced

4 x 175 g/6 oz thick cod fillets
  with skin

freshly cooked vegtables, to serve

1   Preheat oven to 180°C/350°F/Gas Mark 4, 10 minutes before cooking. Crush the garlic, saffron and a pinch of salt in a pestle and mortar to form a paste. Place in a blender with the egg yolk and blend for 30 seconds. With the motor running, slowly add the olive oil in a thin, steady stream until the mayonnaise is smooth and thick. Spoon into a small bowl and stir in the lemon juice. Cover and leave in the refrigerator until required.

2   Combine the olive oil, garlic, red onion, rosemary and thyme for the marinade and leave to infuse for about 10 minutes.

3   Place the sprigs of rosemary and slices of lemon in the bottom of a lightly oiled roasting tin. Add the cod, skinned-side up. Pour over the prepared marinade and leave to marinate in the refrigerator for 15–20 minutes. Bake in the preheated oven for 15–20 minutes, or until the cod is cooked and the flesh flakes easily with a fork. Leave the cod to rest for 1 minute before serving with the saffron aïoli and vegetables.

1

2

3

Foil–baked Fish

INGREDIENTS

Serves 4

For the tomato sauce:

125 ml/4 fl oz olive oil

4 garlic cloves, peeled and
  finely chopped

4 shallots, peeled and finely chopped

400 g can chopped Italian tomatoes

2 tbsp freshly chopped
  flat-leaf parsley

3 tbsp basil leaves

salt and freshly ground black pepper

700 g/1½ lb red mullet, bass or
  haddock fillets

450 g/1 lb live mussels

4 squids

8 large raw prawns

2 tbsp olive oil

3 tbsp dry white wine

3 tbsp freshly chopped basil leaves

lemon wedges, to garnish

HELPFUL HINT

This is an excellent basic sauce. Make a large batch and keep covered in the refrigerator or freeze for up to 2 months. Thaw completely and reheat gently before using.

1 Preheat oven to 180°C/350°F/Gas Mark 4, 10 minutes before cooking. Heat the olive oil and gently fry the garlic and shallots for 2 minutes. Stir in the tomatoes and simmer for 10 minutes, breaking the tomatoes down with the wooden spoon. Add the parsley and basil, season to taste with salt and pepper and cook for a further 2 minutes. Reserve and keep warm.

2 Lightly rinse the fish fillets and cut into 4 portions. Scrub the mussels thoroughly, removing the beard and any barnacles from the shells. Discard any mussels that are open. Clean the squid and cut into rings. Peel the prawns and remove the thin black intestinal vein that runs down the back.

3 Cut 4 large pieces of tinfoil, then place them on a large baking sheet and brush with olive oil. Place 1 fish portion in the centre of each piece of tinfoil. Close the tinfoil to form parcels. and bake in the preheated oven for 10 minutes, then remove.

4 Carefully open up the parcels and add the mussels, squid and prawns. Pour in the wine and spoon over a little of the tomato sauce. Sprinkle with the basil leaves and return to the oven and bake for 5 minutes, or until cooked thoroughly. Disgard any unopened mussels, then garnish with lemon wedges and serve with the extra tomato sauce.

1

3

4

Roasted Monkfish with Parma Ham

INGREDIENTS

Serves 4

700 g/1½ lb monkfish tail
sea salt and freshly ground
  black pepper
4 bay leaves
4 slices fontina cheese, rind removed
8 slices Parma ham
225 g/8 oz angel hair pasta
50 g/2 oz butter
the zest and juice of 1 lemon
sprigs of fresh coriander, to garnish

To serve:
chargrilled courgettes
chargrilled tomatoes

HELPFUL HINT

Monkfish is also sold in boneless fillets, sometimes called loins. Remove the skin from the fish before cooking and if cubes or strips are required, remove the central bone.

1 Preheat oven to 200°C/400°F/Gas Mark 6, 15 minutes before cooking. Discard any skin from the monkfish tail and cut away and discard the central bone. Cut the fish into 4 equal-sized pieces and season to taste with salt and pepper and lay a bay leaf on each fillet, along with a slice of cheese.

2 Wrap each fillet with 2 slices of the Parma ham, so that the fish is covered completely. Tuck the ends of the Parma ham in and secure with a cocktail stick.

3 Lightly oil a baking sheet and place in the preheated oven for a few minutes. Place the fish on the preheated baking sheet, then place in the oven and cook for 12–15 minutes.

4 Bring a large saucepan of lightly salted water to the boil, then slowly add the pasta and cook for 5 minutes until 'al dente', or according to packet directions. Drain, reserving 2 tablespoons of the pasta-cooking liquor. Return the pasta to the saucepan and add the reserved pasta liquor, butter, lemon zest and juice. Toss until the pasta is well coated and glistening.

5 Twirl the pasta into small nests on 4 warmed serving plates and top with the monkfish parcels. Garnish with sprigs of coriander and serve with chargrilled courgettes and tomatoes.

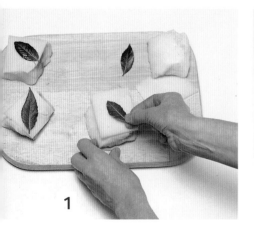

1

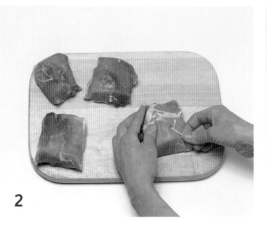

2

5

Mussels Arrabbiata

INGREDIENTS

Serves 4

1.8 kg/4 lb mussels
3–4 tbsp olive oil
1 large onion, peeled and sliced
4 garlic cloves, peeled and
  finely chopped
1 red chilli, deseeded and
  finely chopped
3 x 400 g cans chopped tomatoes
150 ml/¼ pint white wine
175 g/6 oz black olives, pitted
  and halved
salt and freshly ground black pepper
2 tbsp freshly chopped parsley
warm crusty bread, to serve

1 Clean the mussels by scrubbing with a small, soft brush, removing the beard and any barnacles from the shells. Discard any mussels that are open or have damaged shells. Place in a large bowl and cover with cold water. Change the water frequently before cooking and leave in the refrigerator until required.

2 Heat the olive oil in a large saucepan and sweat the onion, garlic and chilli until soft, but not coloured. Add the tomatoes and bring to the boil, then simmer for 15 minutes.

3 Add the white wine to the tomato sauce, bring the sauce to the boil and add the mussels. Cover and carefully shake the pan. Cook the mussels for 5–7 minutes, or until the shells have opened.

4 Add the olives to the pan and cook uncovered for about 5 minutes to warm through. Season to taste with salt and pepper and sprinkle in the chopped parsley. Discard any mussels that have not opened and serve immediately with lots of warm crusty bread.

FOOD FACT

Arrabbiata sauce is a classic Italian tomato-based sauce, usually containing onions, peppers, garlic and fresh herbs. It needs slow simmering to bring out the flavour and is excellent with meat, poultry and pasta as well as seafood.

2

3

4

Tuna Cannelloni

INGREDIENTS

Serves 4

1 tbsp olive oil
6 spring onions, trimmed and
    finely sliced
1 sweet Mediterranean red pepper,
    deseeded and finely chopped
200 g can tuna in brine
250 g tub ricotta cheese
zest and juice of 1 lemon
1 tbsp freshly snipped chives
salt and freshly ground black pepper
8 dried cannelloni tubes
1 medium egg, beaten
125 g/4 oz cottage cheese
150 ml/¼ pint natural yogurt
pinch of freshly grated nutmeg
50 g/2 oz mozzarella cheese, grated
tossed green salad, to serve

1 Preheat oven to 180°C/375°F/Gas Mark 5, 10 minutes before cooking. Heat the olive oil in a frying pan and cook the spring onions and pepper until soft. Remove from the pan with a slotted draining spoon and place in large bowl.

2 Drain the tuna, then stir into the spring onions and pepper. Beat the ricotta cheese with the lemon zest and juice, and the snipped chives and season to taste with salt and pepper until soft and blended. Add to the tuna and mix together. If the mixture is still a little stiff, add a little extra lemon juice.

3 With a teaspoon, carefully spoon the mixture into the cannelloni tubes, then lay the filled tubes in a lightly oiled shallow ovenproof dish. Beat the egg, cottage cheese, natural yogurt and nutmeg together and pour over the cannelloni. Sprinkle with the grated mozzarella cheese and bake in the preheated oven for 15–20 minutes, or until the topping is golden brown and bubbling. Serve immediately with a tossed green salad.

HELPFUL HINT

It may seem tempting to part cook the cannelloni tubes before stuffing them but this makes them too slippery to handle. The moisture in the sauce is sufficient to cook them thoroughly while they are baking in the oven.

1

2

3

Seared Tuna with Italian Salsa

INGREDIENTS

Serves 4

4 x 175 g/6 oz tuna or
    swordfish steaks
salt and freshly ground black pepper
3 tbsp Pernod
2 tbsp olive oil
zest and juice of 1 lemon
2 tsp fresh thyme leaves
2 tsp fennel seeds, lightly roasted
4 sun-dried tomatoes, chopped
1 tsp dried chilli flakes
assorted salad leaves, to serve

For the salsa:

1 white onion, peeled and
    finely chopped
2 tomatoes, deseeded and sliced
2 tbsp freshly shredded basil leaves
1 red chilli, deseeded and finely sliced
3 tbsp extra-virgin olive oil
2 tsp balsamic vinegar
1 tsp caster sugar

1   Wipe the fish and season lightly with salt and pepper, then place
    in a shallow dish. Mix together the Pernod, olive oil, lemon zest
    and juice, thyme, fennel seeds, sun-dried tomatoes and chilli flakes
    and pour over the fish. Cover lightly and leave to marinate in a
    cool place for 1–2 hours, occasionally spooning the marinade over
    the fish.

2   Meanwhile, mix all the ingredients for the salsa together in a small
    bowl. Season to taste with salt and pepper, then cover and leave for
    about 30 minutes to allow all the flavours to develop.

3   Lightly oil a griddle pan and heat until hot. When the pan is very
    hot, drain the fish, reserving the marinade. Cook the fish for 3–4
    minutes on each side, taking care not to overcook them – the tuna
    steaks should be a little pink inside. Pour any remaining marinade
    into a small saucepan, bring to the boil and boil for 1 minute. Serve
    the steaks hot with the marinade, chilled salsa and a few assorted
    salad leaves.

1

2

3

Mediterranean Fish Stew

INGREDIENTS

Serves 4–6

4 tbsp olive oil

1 onion, peeled and finely sliced

5 garlic cloves, peeled and
  finely sliced

1 fennel bulb, trimmed and
  finely chopped

3 celery sticks, trimmed and
  finely chopped

400 g can chopped tomatoes with
  Italian herbs

1 tbsp freshly chopped oregano

1 bay leaf

zest and juice of 1 orange

1 tsp saffron strands

750 ml/1¼ pints fish stock

3 tbsp dry vermouth

salt and freshly ground black pepper

225 g/8 oz thick haddock fillets

225 g/8 oz sea bass or bream fillets

225 g/8 oz raw tiger prawns, peeled

crusty bread, to serve

1 Heat the olive oil in a large saucepan. Add the onion, garlic, fennel and celery and cook over a low heat for 15 minutes, stirring frequently until the vegetables are soft and just beginning to turn brown.

2 Add the canned tomatoes with their juice, oregano, bay leaf, orange zest and juice with the saffron strands. Bring to the boil, then reduce the heat and simmer for 5 minutes. Add the fish stock, vermouth and season to taste with salt and pepper. Bring to the boil. Reduce the heat and simmer for 20 minutes.

3 Wipe or rinse the haddock and bass fillets and remove as many of the bones as possible. Place on a chopping board and cut into 5 cm/2 inch cubes. Add to the saucepan and cook for 3 minutes. Add the prawns and cook for a further 5 minutes. Adjust the seasoning to taste and serve with crusty bread.

1

2

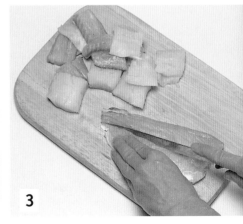

3

Plaice with Parmesan & Anchovies

INGREDIENTS

Serves 4–6

4 plaice fillets
4 anchovy fillets, finely chopped
450 g/1 lb spinach, rinsed
3 firm tomatoes, sliced
200 ml/7 fl oz double cream
5 slices of olive ciabatta bread
50 g/2 oz wild rocket
8 tbsp Parmesan cheese, grated
freshly cooked pasta, to serve

HELPFUL HINT

Anchovies can either be preserved in oil (usually olive oil) or salt. If you buy them preserved in oil, simply lift them from the oil and drain on kitchen paper before using. If you buy salted anchovies, soak them in several changes of water to remove most of the salt before using. Also, season dishes containing anchovies carefully to avoid oversalting.

1 Preheat oven to 220°C/425°F/Gas Mark 7, 15 minutes before cooking. Put the plaice on a chopping board and holding the tail, strip off the skin from both sides. With a filleting knife, fillet the fish, then wipe and reserve.

2 Place the fillets on a large chopping board, skinned-side up and halve lengthways along the centre. Dot each one with some of the chopped anchovies, then roll up from the thickest end and reserve.

3 Pour boiling water over the spinach, leave for 2 minutes, drain, squeezing out as much moisture as possible, then place in the base of an ovenproof dish. Arrange the tomatoes on top of the spinach. Arrange the rolled-up fillets standing up in the dish and pour over the cream.

4 Place the ciabatta and rocket in a food processor and blend until finely chopped, then stir in the grated Parmesan cheese.

5 Sprinkle the topping over the fish and bake in the preheated oven for 8–10 minutes,or until the fish is cooked and has lost its translucency and the topping is golden brown. Serve with freshly cooked pasta.

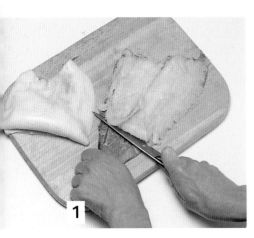

1

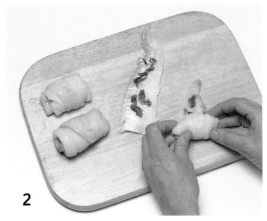

2

3

Grilled Red Mullet with Orange & Anchovy Sauce

INGREDIENTS

Serves 4

2 oranges

4 x 175 g/6 oz red mullet, cleaned
and descaled

salt and freshly ground black pepper

4 sprigs of fresh rosemary

1 lemon, sliced

2 tbsp olive oil

2 garlic cloves, peeled and crushed

6 anchovies fillets in oil, drained and
roughly chopped

2 tsp freshly chopped rosemary

1 tsp lemon juice

1 Preheat the grill and line the grill rack with tinfoil just before cooking. Peel the oranges with a sharp knife, over a bowl in order to catch the juice. Cut into thin slices and reserve. If necessary, make up the juice to 150 ml/¼ pint with extra juice.

2 Place the fish on a chopping board and make 2 diagonal slashes across the thickest part of both sides of the fish. Season well, both inside and out, with salt and pepper. Tuck a rosemary sprig and a few lemon slices inside the cavity of each fish. Brush the fish with a little of the olive oil and then cook under the preheated grill for 4–5 minutes on each side. The flesh should just fall away from the bone.

3 Heat the remaining oil in a saucepan and gently fry the garlic and anchovies for 3–4 minutes. Do not allow to brown. Add the chopped rosemary and plenty of black pepper. The anchovies will be salty enough, so do not add any salt. Stir in the orange slices with their juice and the lemon juice. Simmer gently until heated through. Spoon the sauce over the red mullet and serve immediately.

HELPFUL HINT

Red mullet is a fairly common fish but size can vary enormously – often only very large fish are available. Substitute with grey mullet or snapper, if necessary.

1

2

3

Grilled Snapper with Roasted Pepper

INGREDIENTS

Serves 4

1 medium red pepper
1 medium green pepper
4–8 snapper fillets, depending
    on size, about 450 g/1 lb
sea salt and freshly ground
    black pepper
1 tbsp olive oil
5 tbsp double cream
125 ml/4 fl oz white wine
1 tbsp freshly chopped dill
sprigs of fresh dill, to garnish
freshly cooked tagliatelle, to serve

1 Preheat the grill to a high heat and line the grill rack with tinfoil. Cut the tops off the peppers and divide into quarters. Remove the seeds and the membrane, then place on the foil-lined grill rack and cook for 8–10 minutes, turning frequently, until the skins have become charred and blackened. Remove from the grill rack, place in a polythene bag and leave until cool. When the peppers are cool, strip off the skin, slice thinly and reserve.

2 Cover the grill rack with another piece of tinfoil, then place the snapper fillets skin-side up on the grill rack. Season to taste with salt and pepper and brush with a little of the olive oil. Cook for 10-12 minutes, turning over once and brushing again with a little olive oil.

3 Pour the cream and wine into a small saucepan, bring to the boil and simmer for about 5 minutes until the sauce has thickened slightly. Add the dill, season to taste and stir in the sliced peppers. Arrange the cooked snapper fillets on warm serving plates and pour over the cream and pepper sauce. Garnish with sprigs of dill and serve immediately with freshly cooked tagliatelle.

TASTY TIP

This dish would be just as tasty with a variety of grilled vegetables – try different coloured peppers, red onions, courgettes and aubergines. Cut into slices or wedges and grill as above. Chop or slice when cool enough to handle.

1

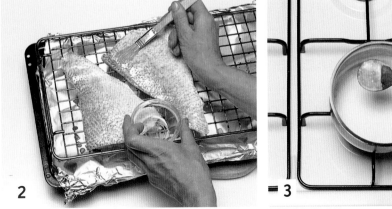

2

3

Pan-fried Salmon with Herb Risotto

INGREDIENTS

Serves 4

4 x 175 g/6 oz salmon fillets
3–4 tbsp plain flour
1 tsp dried mustard powder
salt and freshly ground black pepper
2 tbsp olive oil
3 shallots, peeled and chopped
225 g/8 oz Arborio rice
150 ml/¼ pint dry white wine
1.4 litres/2½ pints vegetable or
   fish stock
50 g/2 oz butter
2 tbsp freshly snipped chives
2 tbsp freshly chopped dill
2 tbsp freshly chopped
   flat-leaf parsley
knob of butter

To garnish:

slices of lemon
sprigs of fresh dill
tomato salad, to serve

1 Wipe the salmon fillets with a clean, damp cloth. Mix together the flour, mustard powder and seasoning on a large plate and use to coat the salmon fillets and reserve.

2 Heat half the olive oil in a large frying pan and fry the shallots for 5 minutes until softened, but not coloured. Add the rice and stir for 1 minute, then slowly add the wine, bring to the boil and boil rapidly until reduced by half.

3 Bring the stock to a gentle simmer, then add to the rice, a ladleful at a time. Cook, stirring frequently, until all the stock has been added and the rice is cooked but still retains a bite. Stir in the butter and freshly chopped herbs and season to taste with salt and pepper.

4 Heat the remaining olive oil and the knob of butter in a large griddle pan, add the salmon fillets and cook for 2–3 minutes on each side, or until cooked. Arrange the herb risotto on warm serving plates and top with the salmon. Garnish with slices of lemon and sprigs of dill and serve immediately with a tomato salad.

1

3

4

Sea Bass in Creamy Watercress & Prosciutto Sauce

INGREDIENTS

Serves 4

75 g/3 oz watercress
450 ml/³/₄ pint fish or chicken stock
150 ml/¹/₄ pint dry white wine
225 g/8 oz tagliatelle pasta
40 g/1¹/₂ oz butter
75 g/3 oz prosciutto ham
2 tbsp plain flour
300 ml/¹/₂ pint single cream
salt and freshly ground black pepper
olive oil, for spraying
4 x 175 g/6 oz sea bass fillets
fresh watercress, to garnish

1. Remove the leaves from the watercress stalks and reserve. Chop the stalks roughly and put in a large pan with the stock. Bring to the boil slowly, cover, and simmer for 20 minutes. Strain, and discard the stalks. Make the stock up to 300 ml/¹/₂ pint with the wine.

2. Bring a large saucepan of lightly salted water to the boil and cook the pasta for 8–10 minutes or until 'al dente'. Drain and reserve.

3. Melt the butter in a saucepan, and cook the prosciutto gently for 3 minutes. Remove with a slotted spoon. Stir the flour into the saucepan and cook on a medium heat for 2 minutes. Remove from the heat and gradually pour in the hot watercress stock, stirring continuously. Return to the heat and bring to the boil, stirring throughout. Simmer for 3 minutes, or until the sauce has thickened and is smooth. Purée the watercress leaves and cream in a food processor then add to the sauce with the prosciutto. Season to taste with salt and pepper, add the pasta, toss lightly and keep warm.

4. Meanwhile, spray a griddle pan lightly with olive oil, then heat until hot. When hot, cook the fillets for 3–4 minutes on each side, or until cooked. Arrange the sea bass on a bed of pasta and drizzle with a little sauce. Garnish with watercress and serve immediately.

HELPFUL HINT

Always wash watercress thoroughly before using, then either dry in a clean tea towel or a salad spinner to remove all the excess moisture.

1

3

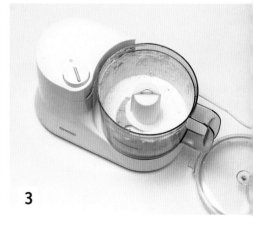
3

Marinated Mackerel with Tomato & Basil Salad

INGREDIENTS

Serves 3

3 mackerel, filleted
3 beefsteak tomatoes, sliced
50 g/2 oz watercress
2 oranges, peeled and segmented
75 g/3 oz mozzarella cheese, sliced
2 tbsp basil leaves, shredded
sprig of fresh basil, to garnish

For the marinade:
juice of 2 lemons
4 tbsp olive oil
4 tbsp basil leaves

For the dressing:
1 tbsp lemon juice
1 tsp Dijon mustard
1 tsp caster sugar
salt and freshly ground black pepper
5 tbsp olive oil

FOOD FACT
Make sure that the fish is absolutely fresh for this dish – use a busy fishmonger, who will have a high turnover and therefore a fresh supply.

1 Remove as many of the fine pin bones as possible from the mackerel fillets, lightly rinse and pat dry with absorbent kitchen paper and place in a shallow dish.

2 Blend the marinade ingredients together and pour over the mackerel fillets. Make sure the marinade has covered the fish completely. Cover and leave in a cool place for at least 8 hours, but preferably overnight. As the fillets marinate, they will loose the translucency and look as if they are cooked.

3 Place the tomatoes, watercress, oranges and mozzarella cheese in a large bowl and toss.

4 To make the dressing, whisk the lemon juice with the mustard, sugar and seasoning in a bowl. Pour over half the dressing, toss again and then arrange on a serving platter. Remove the mackerel from the marinade, cut into bite-sized pieces and sprinkle with the shredded basil. Arrange on top of the salad, drizzle over the remaining dressing, scatter with basil leaves and garnish with a basil sprig. Serve.

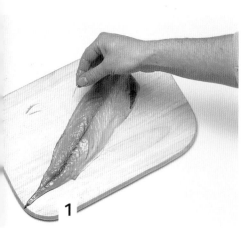

1

2

4

Seafood Special

INGREDIENTS

Serves 3

2 tbsp olive oil
4 garlic cloves, peeled
125 g/4 oz squid, cut into rings
300 ml/½ pint medium-dry
    white wine
400 g can chopped tomatoes
2 tbsp fresh parsley, finely chopped
225 g/8 oz live mussels, cleaned and
    beards removed
125 g/4 oz monkfish fillet
125 g/4 oz fresh tuna
4 slices of Italian bread

To garnish:

225 g/8 oz large, unpeeled
    prawns, cooked
4 langoustines, cooked
3 tbsp freshly chopped parsley

1 Heat the olive oil in a saucepan. Chop half of the garlic, add to the saucepan and gently cook for 1–2 minutes. Add the squid, 150 ml/ ¼ pint of the wine together with the tomatoes and simmer for 10–15 minutes.

2 Chop the remaining garlic and place with the remaining wine and 2 tablespoons of the parsley in another saucepan. Add the cleaned mussels to the pan, cover and cook for 7–8 minutes. Discard any mussels that have not opened, then remove the remaining mussels with a slotted spoon and add to the squid and tomato mixture. Reserve the liquor.

3 Cut the monkfish and tuna into chunks and place in the saucepan with the mussels' cooking liquor. Simmer for about 5 minutes, or until the fish is just tender.

4 Mix all the cooked fish and shellfish, with the exception of the prawns and langoustines, with the tomato mixture and cooking liquor in a large saucepan. Heat everything through until piping hot.

5 Toast the slices of bread and place in the base of a large, shallow serving dish.

6 Pour the fish mixture over the toasted bread and garnish with the prawns, langoustines and chopped parsley. Serve immediately.

TASTY TIP

This dish requires a well-flavoured bread – use a good-quality ciabatta or Pugliese loaf from an Italian delicatessen.

1

3

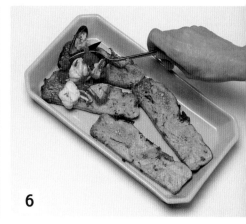
6

Oven-roasted Vegetables with Sausages

INGREDIENTS

Serves 4

2 medium aubergines, trimmed

3 medium courgettes, trimmed

4 tbsp olive oil

6 garlic cloves

8 Tuscan-style sausages

4 plum tomatoes

2 x 300 g cans cannellini beans

salt and freshly ground black pepper

1 bunch of fresh basil, torn into
   coarse pieces

4 tbsp Parmesan cheese, grated

1 Preheat oven to 200°C/400°F/Gas Mark 6, 15 minutes before cooking. Cut the aubergines and courgettes into bite-sized chunks. Place the olive oil in a large roasting tin and heat in the preheated oven for 3 minutes, or until very hot. Add the aubergines, courgettes and garlic cloves, then stir until coated in the hot oil and cook in the oven for 10 minutes.

2 Remove the roasting tin from the oven and stir. Lightly prick the sausages, add to the roasting tin and return to the oven. Continue to roast for a further 20 minutes, turning once during cooking, until the vegetables are tender and the sausages are golden brown.

3 Meanwhile, roughly chop the plum tomatoes and drain the cannellini beans. Remove the sausages from the oven and stir in the tomatoes and cannellini beans. Season to taste with salt and pepper, then return to the oven for 5 minutes, or until heated thoroughly.

4 Scatter over the basil leaves and sprinkle with plenty of Parmesan cheese and extra freshly ground black pepper. Serve immediately.

HELPFUL HINT

Although it is worth seeking out Tuscan-style sausages for this dish, a good alternative would be to use Toulouse sausages instead, as these are more readily available from large supermarkets and from selected butchers.

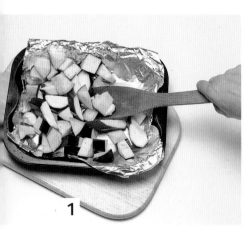

1

2

3

Hot Salami & Vegetable Gratin

INGREDIENTS

Serves 4

350 g/12 oz carrots
175 g/6 oz fine green beans
250 g/9 oz asparagus tips
175 g/6 oz frozen peas
225 g/8 oz Italian salami
1 tbsp olive oil
1 tbsp freshly chopped mint
25 g/1 oz butter
150 g/5 oz baby spinach leaves
150 ml/¼ pint double cream
salt and freshly ground black pepper
1 small or ½ an olive ciabatta loaf
75 g/3 oz Parmesan cheese, grated
green salad, to serve

1 Preheat oven to 200°C/400°F/Gas Mark 6. Peel and slice the carrots, trim the beans and asparagus and reserve. Cook the carrots in a saucepan of lightly salted, boiling water for 5 minutes. Add the remaining vegetables, except the spinach, and cook for about a further 5 minutes, or until tender. Drain and place in an ovenproof dish.

2 Discard any skin from the outside of the salami, if necessary, then chop roughly. Heat the oil in a frying pan and fry the salami for 4–5 minutes, stirring occasionally, until golden. Using a slotted spoon, transfer the salami to the ovenproof dish and scatter over the mint.

3 Add the butter to the frying pan and cook the spinach for 1–2 minutes, or until just wilted. Stir in the double cream and season well with salt and pepper. Spoon the mixture over the vegetables.

4 Whiz the ciabatta loaf in a food processor to make breadcrumbs. Stir in the Parmesan cheese and sprinkle over the vegetables. Bake in the preheated oven for 20 minutes, until golden and heated through. Serve with a green salad.

TASTY TIP

Prepare this dish ahead up to the end of step 3 and refrigerate until ready to cook, then top with breadcrumbs and bake, adding about 5 minutes to the final cooking time.

1

2

4

Antipasto Penne

INGREDIENTS

Serves 4

3 medium courgettes, trimmed

4 plum tomatoes

175 g/6 oz Italian ham

2 tbsp olive oil

salt and freshly ground black pepper

350 g/12 oz dried penne pasta

285 g jar antipasto

125 g/4 oz mozzarella cheese, drained
  and diced

125 g/4 oz Gorgonzola
  cheese, crumbled

3 tbsp freshly chopped
  flat-leaf parsley

FOOD FACT

The term 'antipasto' refers to the course served before the pasto or meal begins and its purpose is to whet the appetite for the following courses. In Italy, these are served in small quantities, though 2 or 3 different dishes may be served at once. There are no rules as to what is a suitable dish for antipasti – there are thousands of regional variations.

1 Preheat the grill just before cooking. Cut the courgettes into thick slices. Rinse the tomatoes and cut into quarters, then cut the ham into strips. Pour the oil into a baking dish and place under the grill for 2 minutes, or until almost smoking. Remove from the grill and stir in the courgettes. Return to the grill and cook for 8 minutes, stirring occasionally. Remove from the grill and add the tomatoes and cook for a further 3 minutes.

2 Add the ham to the baking dish and cook under the grill for 4 minutes, until all the vegetables are charred and the ham is brown. Season to taste with salt and pepper.

3 Meanwhile, plunge the pasta into a large saucepan of lightly salted, boiling water, return to a rolling boil, stir and cook for 8 minutes, or until 'al dente'. Drain well and return to the saucepan.

4 Stir the antipasto into the vegetables and cook under the grill for 2 minutes, or until heated through. Add the cooked pasta and toss together gently with the remaining ingredients. Grill for a further 4 minutes, then serve immediately.

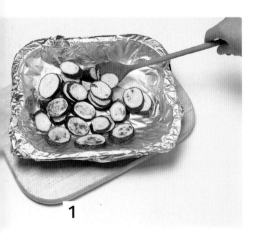

1

2

4

Italian Risotto

INGREDIENTS

Serves 4

1 onion, peeled

2 garlic cloves, peeled

1 tbsp olive oil

125 g/4 oz Italian salami or
  speck, chopped

125 g/4 oz asparagus

350 g/12 oz risotto rice

300 ml/½ pt dry white wine

1 litre/1¾ pints chicken
  stock, warmed

125g/4 oz frozen broad
  beans, defrosted

125g/4 oz Dolcelatte cheese, diced

3 tbsp freshly chopped mixed herbs,
  such as parsley and basil

salt and freshly ground black pepper

1 Chop the onion and garlic and reserve. Heat the olive oil in a large frying pan and cook the salami for 3–5 minutes, or until golden. Using a slotted spoon, transfer to a plate and keep warm. Add the asparagus and stir-fry for 2–3 minutes, until just wilted. Transfer to the plate with the salami. Add the onion and garlic and cook for 5 minutes, or until softened.

2 Add the rice to the pan and cook for about 2 minutes. Add the wine, bring to the boil, then simmer, stirring until the wine has been absorbed. Add half the stock and return to the boil. Simmer, stirring until the liquid has been absorbed.

3 Add half of the remaining stock and the broad beans to the rice mixture. Bring to the boil, then simmer for a further 5–10 minutes, or until all of the liquid has been absorbed.

4 Add the remaining stock, bring to the boil, then simmer until all the liquid is absorbed and the rice is tender. Stir in the remaining ingredients until the cheese has just melted. Serve immediately.

FOOD FACT

Cheese is a common constituent in the making of risotto and in fact helps to provide some of its creamy texture. Usually Parmesan cheese is added at the end of cooking but here a good-quality Dolcelatte is used instead.

1

2

4

Pan–fried Beef with Creamy Mushrooms

INGREDIENTS

Serves 4

225 g/8 oz shallots, peeled
2 garlic cloves, peeled
2 tbsp olive oil
4 medallions of beef
4 plum tomatoes
125 g/4 oz flat mushrooms
3 tbsp brandy
150 ml/¼ pint red wine
salt and freshly ground black pepper
4 tbsp double cream

To serve:

baby new potatoes
freshly cooked green beans

1 Cut the shallots in half if large, then chop the garlic. Heat the oil in a large frying pan and cook the shallots for about 8 minutes, stirring occasionally, until almost softened. Add the garlic and beef and cook for 8–10 minutes, turning once during cooking until the meat is browned all over. Using a slotted spoon, transfer the beef to a plate and keep warm.

2 Rinse the tomatoes and cut into eighths, then wipe the mushrooms and slice. Add to the pan and cook for 5 minutes, stirring frequently until the mushrooms have softened.

3 Pour in the brandy and heat through. Draw the pan off the heat and carefully ignite. Allow the flames to subside. Pour in the wine, return to the heat and bring to the boil. Boil until reduced by one-third. Draw the pan off the heat, season to taste with salt and pepper, add the cream and stir.

4 Arrange the beef on serving plates and spoon over the sauce. Serve with baby new potatoes and a few green beans.

HELPFUL HINT

To prepare medallions of beef, buy a piece of fillet weighing approximately 700 g/1½ lb. Cut crosswise into 4 pieces.

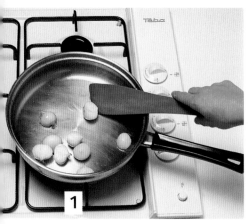
1

2

3

Oven–baked Pork Balls with Peppers

INGREDIENTS

Serves 4

For the garlic bread:
2–4 garlic cloves, peeled
50 g/2 oz butter, softened
1 tbsp freshly chopped parsley
2–3 tsp lemon juice
1 focaccia loaf

For the pork balls:
450 g/1 lb fresh pork mince
4 tbsp freshly chopped basil
2 garlic cloves, peeled and chopped
3 sun-dried tomatoes, chopped
salt and freshly ground black pepper
3 tbsp olive oil
1 medium red pepper, deseeded and
    cut into chunks
1 medium green pepper, deseeded
    and cut into chunks
1 medium yellow pepper, deseeded
    and cut into chunks
225 g/8 oz cherry tomatoes
2 tbsp balsamic vinegar

HELPFUL HINT
Prepare the garlic butter ahead to
the end of step 1. Refrigerate for
up to 1 week or freeze for up to
2 months.

1 Preheat oven to 200°C/400°F/Gas Mark 6, 15 minutes before cooking. Crush the garlic, then blend with the softened butter, the parsley and enough lemon juice to give a soft consistency. Shape into a roll, wrap in baking parchment paper and chill in the refrigerator for at least 30 minutes.

2 Mix together the pork, basil, 1 chopped garlic clove, sun-dried tomatoes and seasoning until well combined. With damp hands, divide the mixture into 16, roll into balls and reserve.

3 Spoon the olive oil in a large roasting tin and place in the preheated oven for about 3 minutes, until very hot. Remove from the heat and stir in the pork balls, the remaining chopped garlic and peppers. Bake for about 15 minutes. Remove from the oven and stir in the cherry tomatoes and season to taste with plenty of salt and pepper. Bake for about a further 20 minutes.

4 Just before the pork balls are ready, slice the bread, toast lightly and spread with the prepared garlic butter. Remove the pork balls from the oven, stir in the vinegar and serve immediately with garlic bread.

1

2

3

Pork Chop Hotpot

INGREDIENTS

Serves 4

4 pork chops
flour for dusting
225 g/8 oz shallots, peeled
2 garlic cloves, peeled
50 g/2 oz sun-dried tomatoes
2 tbsp olive oil
400 g can plum tomatoes
150 ml/¼ pint red wine
150 ml/¼ pint chicken stock
3 tbsp tomato purée
2 tbsp freshly chopped oregano
salt and freshly ground black pepper
fresh oregano leaves, to garnish

To serve:

freshly cooked new potatoes
French beans

1   Preheat oven to 190°C/375°F/Gas Mark 5, 10 minutes before cooking. Trim the pork chops, removing any excess fat, wipe with a clean, damp cloth, then dust with a little flour and reserve. Cut the shallots in half if large. Chop the garlic and slice the sun-dried tomatoes.

2   Heat the olive oil in a large casserole dish and cook the pork chops for about 5 minutes, turning occasionally during cooking, until browned all over. Using a slotted spoon, carefully lift out of the dish and reserve. Add the shallots and cook for 5 minutes, stirring occasionally.

3   Return the pork chops to the casserole dish and scatter with the garlic and sun-dried tomatoes, then pour over the can of tomatoes with their juice.

4   Blend the red wine, stock and tomato purée together and add the chopped oregano. Season to taste with salt and pepper, then pour over the pork chops and bring to a gentle boil. Cover with a close-fitting lid and cook in the preheated oven for 1 hour, or until the pork chops are tender. Adjust the seasoning to taste, then scatter with a few oregano leaves and serve immediately with freshly cooked potatoes and French beans.

TASTY TIP

Choose bone-in chops for this recipe. Remove any excess fat and rind before cooking.

Rabbit Italian

INGREDIENTS

Serves 4

450 g/1 lb diced rabbit, thawed
    if frozen
6 rashers streaky bacon
1 garlic clove, peeled
1 onion, peeled
1 carrot, peeled
1 celery stalk
25 g/1 oz butter
2 tbsp olive oil
400 g can chopped tomatoes
150 ml/¼ pint red wine
salt and freshly ground black pepper
125 g/4 oz mushrooms

To serve:
freshly cooked pasta
green salad

1   Trim the rabbit if necessary. Chop the bacon and reserve. Chop the garlic and onion and slice the carrot thinly, then trim the celery and chop.

2   Heat the butter and 1 tablespoon of the oil in a large saucepan and brown the rabbit for 5 minutes, stirring frequently, until sealed all over. Transfer the rabbit to a plate and reserve.

3   Add the garlic, onion, bacon, carrot and celery to the saucepan and cook for a further 5 minutes, stirring occasionally, until softened, then return the rabbit to the saucepan and pour over the tomatoes with their juice and the wine. Season to taste with salt and pepper. Bring to the boil, cover, reduce the heat and simmer for 45 minutes.

4   Meanwhile, wipe the mushrooms and if large, cut in half. Heat the remaining oil in a small frying pan and sauté the mushrooms for 2 minutes. Drain, then add to the rabbit and cook for 15 minutes, or until the rabbit is tender. Season to taste and serve immediately with freshly cooked pasta and a green salad.

HELPFUL HINT
If you prefer to buy a whole rabbit, have your butcher joint it for you into 8 pieces. The method and cooking time will remain the same.

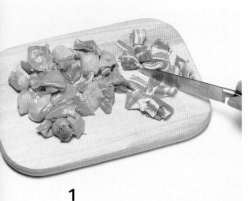
1

2

3

Roasted Lamb with Rosemary & Garlic

INGREDIENTS

Serves 6

1.6 kg/3½ lb leg of lamb
8 garlic cloves, peeled
few sprigs of fresh rosemary
salt and freshly ground black pepper
4 slices pancetta
4 tbsp olive oil
4 tbsp red wine vinegar
900 g/2 lb potatoes
1 large onion
sprigs of fresh rosemary, to garnish
freshly cooked ratatouille, to serve

HELPFUL HINT

If you are unable to get a leg of lamb weighing exactly 1.6 kg/ 3½ lb, calculate the cooking time as follows: 20 minutes per 450 g/ 1 lb plus 30 minutes for rare, 25 minutes per 450 g/1 lb plus 30 minutes for medium and 30 minutes per 450 g/1 lb plus 30 minutes for well-done.

1 Preheat oven to 200°C/400°F/Gas Mark 6, 15 minutes before roasting. Wipe the leg of lamb with a clean damp cloth, then place the lamb in a large roasting tin. With a sharp knife, make small, deep incisions into the meat. Cut 2–3 garlic cloves into small slivers, then insert with a few small sprigs of rosemary into the lamb. Season to taste with salt and pepper and cover the lamb with the slices of pancetta.

2 Drizzle over 1 tablespoon of the olive oil and lay a few more rosemary sprigs across the lamb. Roast in the preheated oven for 30 minutes, then pour over the vinegar.

3 Peel the potatoes and cut into large dice. Peel the onion and cut into thick wedges then thickly slice the remaining garlic. Arrange around the lamb. Pour the remaining olive oil over the potatoes, then reduce the oven temperature to 180°C/ 350°F/Gas Mark 4 and roast for a further 1 hour, or until the lamb is tender. Garnish with fresh sprigs of rosemary and serve immediately with the roast potatoes and ratatouille.

1

2

3

Braised Lamb with Broad Beans

INGREDIENTS

Serves 4

700 g/1½ lb lamb, cut into
  large chunks
1 tbsp plain flour
1 onion
2 garlic cloves
1 tbsp olive oil
400 g can chopped tomatoes
  with basil
300 ml/½ pint lamb stock
2 tbsp freshly chopped thyme
2 tbsp freshly chopped oregano
salt and freshly ground black pepper
150 g/5 oz frozen broad beans
fresh oregano, to garnish
creamy mashed potatoes, to serve

TASTY TIP

If you want to use fresh broad beans in season, you will need about 450 g/1 lb of beans in their pods for this recipe. If you prefer to peel the beans, plunge them first into boiling salted water for about 30 seconds, drain and refresh under cold water. The skins will come off very easily.

1 Trim the lamb, discarding any fat or gristle, then place the flour in a polythene bag, add the lamb and toss until coated thoroughly. Peel and slice the onion and garlic and reserve. Heat the olive oil in a heavy-based saucepan and when hot, add the lamb and cook, stirring until the meat is sealed and browned all over. Using a slotted spoon transfer the lamb to a plate and reserve.

2 Add the onion and garlic to the saucepan and cook for 3 minutes, stirring frequently until softened, then return the lamb to the saucepan. Add the chopped tomatoes with their juice, the stock, the chopped thyme and oregano to the pan and season to taste with salt and pepper. Bring to the boil, then cover with a close-fitting lid, reduce the heat and simmer for 1 hour.

3 Add the broad beans to the lamb and simmer for 20–30 minutes, or until the lamb is tender. Garnish with fresh oregano and serve with creamy mashed potatoes.

Spaghetti Bolognese

INGREDIENTS

Serves 4

1 carrot

2 celery stalks

1 onion

2 garlic cloves

450 g/1 lb lean minced beef steak

225 g/8 oz smoked streaky
  bacon, chopped

1 tbsp plain flour

150 ml//₄ pint red wine

379 g can chopped tomatoes

2 tbsp tomato purée

2 tsp dried mixed herbs

salt and freshly ground black pepper

pinch of sugar

350 g/12 oz spaghetti

sprigs of fresh oregano, to garnish

shavings of Parmesan cheese,
  to serve

TASTY TIP

This is an ideal sauce to use in a baked lasagne. Layer up the sauce with sheets of lasagne and top with a bechamel sauce and Parmesan cheese. Bake for 30–40 minutes in a preheated oven 190°C/375°F/Gas Mark 5, or until bubbling and the top is golden.

1 Peel and chop the carrot, trim and chop the celery, then peel and chop the onion and garlic. Heat a large non-stick frying pan and sauté the beef and bacon for 5–10 minutes, stirring occasionally, until browned. Add the prepared vegetables to the frying pan and cook for about 3 minutes, or until softened, stirring occasionally.

2 Add the flour and cook for 1 minute. Stir in the red wine, tomatoes, tomato purée, mixed herbs, seasoning to taste and sugar. Bring to the boil, then cover and simmer for 45 minutes, stirring occasionally.

3 Meanwhile, bring a large saucepan of lightly salted water to the boil and cook the spaghetti for 10–12 minutes, or until 'al dente'. Drain well and divide between 4 serving plates. Spoon over the sauce, garnish with a few sprigs of oregano and serve immediately with plenty of Parmesan shavings.

Meatballs with Olives

INGREDIENTS

Serves 4

250 g/9 oz shallots, peeled
2–3 garlic cloves, peeled and chopped
450 g/1 lb minced beef steak
2 tbsp fresh white or wholemeal
  breadcrumbs
3 tbsp freshly chopped basil
salt and freshly ground black pepper
2 tbsp olive oil
5 tbsp ready-made pesto sauce
5 tbsp mascarpone cheese
50 g/2 oz pitted black olives, halved
275 g/10 oz thick pasta noodles
freshly chopped flat-leaf parsley
sprigs of fresh flat-leaf parsley,
  to garnish
freshly grated Parmesan cheese,
  to serve

HELPFUL HINT

To stone olives, make a cut lengthways around the olive, then place on a chopping board with the cut facing upwards. Put the side of the knife (with the blade facing away from you) on top of the olive and tap sharply with your hand. The stone should come away leaving the olive in 2 pieces.

1 Chop 2 of the shallots finely and place in a bowl with the garlic, beef, breadcrumbs, basil and seasoning to taste. With damp hands, bring the mixture together and shape into small balls about the size of an apricot.

2 Heat the olive oil in a frying pan and cook the meatballs for 8–10 minutes, turning occasionally, until browned and the beef is tender. Remove and drain on absorbent kitchen paper.

3 Slice the remaining shallots, add to the pan and cook for 5 minutes, until softened. Blend the pesto and mascarpone together, then stir into the pan with the olives. Bring to the boil, reduce the heat and return the meatballs to the pan. Simmer for 5–8 minutes, or until the sauce has thickened and the meatballs are cooked thoroughly.

4 Meanwhile, bring a large saucepan of lightly salted water to the boil and cook the noodles for 8–10 minutes, or 'al dente'. Drain the noodles, reserving 2 tablespoons of the cooking liquor. Return the noodles to the pan with the cooking liquor and pour in the sauce. Stir the noodles, then sprinkle with chopped parsley. Garnish with a few sprigs of parsley and serve immediately with grated Parmesan cheese.

1

2

3

Lasagne

INGREDIENTS

Serves 4

450 g/1 lb lean minced beef steak
175 g/6 oz pancetta or smoked
  streaky bacon, chopped
1 large onion, peeled and chopped
2 celery stalks, trimmed and chopped
125 g/4 oz button mushrooms, wiped
  and chopped
2 garlic cloves, peeled and chopped
90 g/3½ oz plain flour
300 ml/½ pint beef stock
1 tbsp freeze-dried mixed herbs
5 tbsp tomato purée
salt and freshly ground black pepper
75 g/3 oz butter
1 tsp English mustard powder
pinch of freshly grated nutmeg
900 ml/1½ pints milk
125 g/4 oz Parmesan cheese, grated
125 g/4 oz Cheddar cheese, grated
8–12 precooked lasagne sheets

To serve:
crusty bread
fresh green salad leaves

1 Preheat oven to 200°C/400°F/Gas Mark 6, 15 minutes before cooking. Cook the beef and pancetta or bacon in a large saucepan for 10 minutes, stirring to break up any lumps. Add the onion, celery and mushrooms and cook for 4 minutes, or until softened slightly.

2 Stir in the garlic and 1 tablespoon of the flour, then cook for 1 minute. Stir in the stock, herbs and tomato purée. Season to taste with salt and pepper. Bring to the boil, then cover, reduce the heat and simmer for 45 minutes.

3 Meanwhile, melt the butter in a small saucepan and stir in the remaining flour, mustard powder and nutmeg, until well blended. Cook for 2 minutes. Remove from the heat and gradually blend in the milk until smooth. Return to the heat and bring to the boil, stirring, until thickened. Gradually stir in half the Parmesan and Cheddar cheeses until melted. Season to taste.

4 Spoon half the meat mixture into the base of a large ovenproof dish. Top with a single layer of pasta. Spread over half the sauce and scatter with half the cheese. Repeat layers finishing with cheese. Bake in the preheated oven for 30 minutes, or until the pasta is cooked and the top is golden brown and bubbly. Serve immediately with crusty bread and a green salad.

2

3

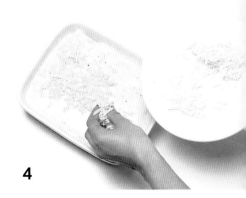

4

Fillet Steaks with Tomato & Garlic Sauce

INGREDIENTS

Serves 4

700 g/1½ lb ripe tomatoes
2 garlic cloves
2 tbsp olive oil
2 tbsp freshly chopped basil
2 tbsp freshly chopped oregano
2 tbsp red wine
salt and freshly ground black pepper
75 g/3 oz pitted black olives, chopped
4 fillet steaks, about 175 g/6 oz each
  in weight
freshly cooked vegetables, to serve

1 Make a small cross on the top of each tomato and place in a large bowl. Cover with boiling water and leave for 2 minutes. Using a slotted spoon, remove the tomatoes and skin carefully. Repeat until all the tomatoes are skinned. Place on a chopping board, cut into quarters, remove the seeds and roughly chop, then reserve.

2 Peel and chop the garlic. Heat half the olive oil in a saucepan and cook the garlic for 30 seconds. Add the chopped tomatoes with the basil, oregano, red wine and season to taste with salt and pepper. Bring to the boil then reduce the heat, cover and simmer for 15 minutes, stirring occasionally, or until the sauce is reduced and thickened. Stir the olives into the sauce and keep warm while cooking the steaks.

3 Meanwhile, lightly oil a griddle pan or heavy-based frying pan with the remaining olive oil and cook the steaks for 2 minutes on each side to seal. Continue to cook the steaks for a further 2–4 minutes, depending on personal preference. Serve the steaks immediately with the garlic sauce and freshly cooked vegetables.

HELPFUL HINT

Fillet steak should be a deep mahogany colour with a good marbling of fat. If the meat is bright red or if the fat is bright white the meat has not been aged properly and will probably be quite tough.

1

2

3

Veal Escalopes with Marsala Sauce

INGREDIENTS

Serves 6

6 veal escalopes, about
 125 g/4 oz each
lemon juice
salt and freshly ground black pepper
6 sage leaves
6 slices prosciutto
2 tbsp olive oil
25 g/1 oz butter
1 onion, peeled and sliced
1 garlic clove, peeled and chopped
2 tbsp Marsala wine
4 tbsp double cream
2 tbsp freshly chopped parsley
sage leaves to garnish
selection of freshly cooked
 vegetables, to serve

1 Place the veal escalopes between sheets of non-pvc clingfilm and using a mallet or rolling pin, pound lightly to flatten out thinly to about 5 mm/¼ inch thickness. Remove the clingfilm and sprinkle the veal escalopes with lemon juice, salt and black pepper.

2 Place a sage leaf in the centre of each escalope. Top with a slice of prosciutto making sure it just fits, then roll up the escalopes enclosing the prosciutto and sage leaves. Secure each escalope with a cocktail stick.

3 Heat the olive oil and butter in a large non-stick frying pan and fry the onions for 5 minutes, or until softened. Add the garlic and rolled escalopes and cook for about 8 minutes, turning occasionally, until the escalopes are browned all over.

4 Add the Marsala wine and cream to the pan and bring to the boil, cover and simmer for 10 minutes, or until the veal is tender. Season to taste and then sprinkle with the parsley. Discard the cocktail sticks and serve immediately with a selection of freshly cooked vegetables.

TASTY TIP

If you prefer not to use veal, substitute with thinly sliced boneless pork loin or thin slices of turkey or chicken breast. Substitute the sage leaves with basil sprigs and try adding sliced cheese, such as Gruyère.

1

2

3

Cannelloni

INGREDIENTS

Serves 4

2 tbsp olive oil

175 g/6 oz fresh pork mince

75 g/3 oz chicken livers, chopped

1 small onion, peeled and chopped

1 garlic clove, peeled and chopped

175 g/6 oz frozen chopped
  spinach, thawed

1 tbsp freeze-dried oregano

pinch of freshly grated nutmeg

salt and freshly ground black pepper

175 g/6 oz ricotta cheese

25 g/1 oz butter

25 g/1 oz plain flour

600 ml/1 pint milk

600 ml/1 pint ready-made
  tomato sauce

16 precooked cannelloni tubes

50 g/2 oz Parmesan cheese, grated

green salad, to serve

TASTY TIP

To make chicken cannelloni, substitute 225 g/8 oz boneless, skinless chicken breast that has been finely chopped in a food processor. Minced chicken is available from large supermarkets.

1 Preheat oven to 190°C/375°F/Gas Mark 5, 10 minutes before cooking. Heat the olive oil in a frying pan and cook the mince and chicken livers for about 5 minutes, stirring occasionally, until browned all over. Break up any lumps if necessary with a wooden spoon.

2 Add the onion and garlic and cook for 4 minutes, until softened. Add the spinach, oregano, nutmeg and season to taste with salt and pepper. Cook until all the liquid has evaporated, then remove the pan from the heat and allow to cool. Stir in the ricotta cheese.

3 Meanwhile, melt the butter in a small saucepan and stir in the plain flour to form a roux. Cook for 2 minutes, stirring occasionally. Remove from the heat and blend in the milk until smooth. Return to the heat and bring to the boil, stirring until the sauce has thickened. Reserve.

4 Spoon a thin layer of the tomato sauce on the base of a large ovenproof dish. Divide the pork filling between the cannelloni tubes. Arrange on top of the tomato sauce. Spoon over the remaining tomato sauce.

5 Pour over the white sauce and sprinkle with the Parmesan cheese. Bake in the preheated oven for 30–35 minutes, or until the cannelloni is tender and the top is golden brown. Serve immediately with a green salad.

1

2

4

Vitello Tonnato
(Veal in Tuna Sauce)

INGREDIENTS

Serves 4

900g/2 lb boned, rolled leg or loin
   of veal
300 ml/½ pint dry white wine
1 onion, peeled and chopped
1 carrot, peeled and chopped
2 celery stalks, trimmed and chopped
1 bay leaf
2 garlic cloves
few sprigs of parsley
salt and freshly ground black pepper
200 g can tuna in oil
2 tbsp capers, drained
6 anchovy fillets
200 ml/7 fl oz mayonnaise
juice of ½ lemon

To garnish:
lemon wedges
capers
black olives

To serve:
fresh green salad leaves
tomato wedges

1   Place the veal in a large bowl and pour over the wine. Add the onion, carrot, celery, bay leaf, garlic cloves, parsley, salt and pepper. Cover tightly and chill overnight in the refrigerator. Transfer the contents of the bowl to a large saucepan, add just enough water to cover the meat. Bring to the boil, cover and simmer for 1–1¼ hours, or until the veal is tender.

2   Remove from the heat and allow the veal to cool in the juices. Using a slotted spoon, transfer the veal to a plate, pat dry with absorbent kitchen paper and reserve.

3   Place the tuna, capers, anchovy fillets, mayonnaise and lemon juice in a food processor or liquidiser and blend until smooth, adding a few spoonfuls of the pan juices to make the sauce of a coating consistency, if necessary. Season to taste with salt and pepper.

4   Using a sharp knife slice the veal thinly and arrange on a large serving platter.

5   Spoon the sauce over the veal. Garnish with lemon wedges, capers and olives. Serve with salad and tomato wedges.

1

3

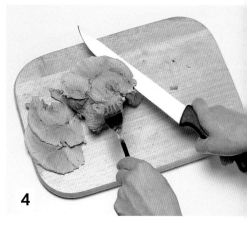

4

Italian Beef Pot Roast

INGREDIENTS

Serves 4

1.8 kg/4 lb brisket of beef
225 g/8 oz small onions, peeled
3 garlic cloves, peeled and chopped
2 celery sticks, trimmed and chopped
2 carrots, peeled and sliced
450 g/1 lb ripe tomatoes
300 ml/½ pint Italian red wine
2 tbsp olive oil
300 ml/½ pint beef stock
1 tbsp tomato purée
2 tsp freeze-dried mixed herbs
salt and freshly ground black pepper
25 g/1 oz butter
25 g/1 oz plain flour
freshly cooked vegetables, to serve

HELPFUL HINT

Most supermarkets do not sell brisket, but good butchers will be able to order it. Brisket is an excellent cut for all kinds of pot roasts, but make sure it is professionally trimmed as it can contain a lot of gristle and fat.

1. Preheat oven to 150°C/300°F/Gas Mark 2, 10 minutes before cooking. Place the beef in a bowl. Add the onions, garlic, celery and carrots. Place the tomatoes in a bowl and cover with boiling water. Allow to stand for 2 minutes and drain. Peel away the skins, discard the seeds and chop, then add to the bowl with the red wine. Cover tightly and marinate in the refrigerator overnight.

2. Lift the marinated beef from the bowl and pat dry with absorbent kitchen paper. Heat the olive oil in a large casserole dish and cook the beef until it is browned all over, then remove from the dish. Drain the vegetables from the marinade, reserving the marinade. Add the vegetables to the casserole dish and fry gently for 5 minutes, stirring occasionally, until all the vegetables are browned.

3. Return the beef to the casserole dish with the marinade, beef stock, tomato purée, mixed herbs and season with salt and pepper. Bring to the boil, then cover and cook in the preheated oven for 3 hours.

4. Using a slotted spoon transfer the beef and any large vegetables to a plate and leave in a warm place. Blend the butter and flour to form a paste. Bring the casserole juices to the boil and then gradually stir in small spoonfuls of the paste. Cook until thickened. Serve with the sauce and a selection of vegetables.

1

2

4

Italian Meatballs in Tomato Sauce

INGREDIENTS

Serves 4

For the tomato sauce:

4 tbsp olive oil

1 large onion, peeled and
  finely chopped

2 garlic cloves, peeled and chopped

400 g can chopped tomatoes

1 tbsp sun-dried tomato paste

1 tbsp dried mixed herbs

150 ml/¼ pint red wine

salt and freshly ground black pepper

For the meatballs:

450 g/1 lb fresh pork mince

50 g/2 oz fresh breadcrumbs

1 medium egg yolk

75 g/3 oz Parmesan cheese, grated

20 small stuffed green olives

freshly snipped chives, to garnish

freshly cooked pasta, to serve

1 To make the tomato sauce, heat half the olive oil in a saucepan and cook half the chopped onion for 5 minutes, until softened.

2 Add the garlic, chopped tomatoes, tomato paste, mixed herbs and red wine to the pan and season to taste with salt and pepper. Stir well until blended. Bring to the boil, then cover and simmer for 15 minutes.

3 To make the meatballs, place the pork, breadcrumbs, remaining onion, egg yolk and half the Parmesan in a large bowl. Season well and mix together with your hands. Divide the mixture into 20 balls.

4 Flatten 1 ball out in the palm of your hands, place an olive in the centre, then squeeze the meat around the olive to enclose completely. Repeat with remaining mixture and olives.

5 Place the meatballs on a baking sheet and cover with clingfilm and chill in the refrigerator for 30 minutes.

6 Heat the remaining oil in a large frying pan and cook the meatballs for 8–10 minutes, turning occasionally, until golden brown. Pour in the sauce and heat through. Sprinkle with chives and the remaining Parmesan. Serve immediately with the freshly cooked pasta.

TASTY TIP

There are many kinds of stuffed olives available; pimento, almond or even anchovy stuffed olives.

Italian Calf Liver

INGREDIENTS

Serves 4

450 g/1 lb calf liver, trimmed
1 onion, peeled and sliced
2 fresh bay leaves, coarsely torn
fresh parsley sprigs
fresh sage leaves
5 black peppercorns, lightly crushed
1 tbsp redcurrant jelly, warmed
4 tbsp walnut or olive oil
4 tbsp red wine vinegar
3 tbsp plain white flour
salt and freshly ground black pepper
2 garlic cloves, peeled and crushed
1 red pepper, deseeded and sliced
1 yellow pepper, deseeded and sliced
3 tbsp sun-dried tomatoes, chopped
150 ml/¼ pint chicken stock
fresh sage leaves, to garnish
diced sauté potatoes, to serve

1 Cut the liver into very thin slices and place in a shallow dish. Sprinkle over the onion, bay leaves, parsley, sage and peppercorns. Blend the redcurrant jelly with 1 tablespoon of the oil and the vinegar. Pour over the liver, cover and leave to marinate for at least 30 minutes. Turn the liver occasionally or spoon over the marinade.

2 Remove the liver from the marinade, strain the liquor and reserve. Season the flour with salt and pepper, then use to coat the liver. Add the remaining oil to a heavy based frying pan, then sauté the garlic and peppers for 5 minutes. Using a slotted spoon, remove from the pan.

3 Add the liver to the pan, turn the heat up to high and cook until the meat is browned on all sides. Return the garlic and peppers to the pan and add the reserved marinade, the sun-dried tomatoes and stock. Bring to the boil, then reduce the heat and simmer for 3–4 minutes, or until the liver is cooked. Add more seasoning, then garnish with a few sage leaves and serve immediately with diced sauté potatoes.

TASTY TIP

Be careful not to overcook the liver in this recipe as it will become tough and dry, even though it is cooked in a sauce. Liver is best left a little pink in the centre.

1

1

3

Saffron Roast Chicken with Crispy Onions

INGREDIENTS

Serves 4–6

1.6 kg/3½ lb oven-ready chicken, preferably free range
75 g/3 oz butter, softened
1 tsp saffron strands, lightly toasted
grated rind of 1 lemon
2 tbsp freshly chopped flat-leaf parsley
2 tbsp extra-virgin olive oil
450 g/1 lb onions, peeled and cut into thin wedges
8–12 garlic cloves, peeled
1 tsp cumin seeds
½ tsp ground cinnamon
50 g/2 oz pine nuts
50 g/2 oz sultanas
salt and freshly ground black pepper
sprig of fresh flat-leaf parsley, to garnish

HELPFUL HINT

Roasting the chicken breast-side down first helps to ensure that the white meat will be moist. Turning the chicken halfway through cooking will give a crisp, golden skin.

1 Preheat oven to 200°C/400°F/Gas Mark 6. Using your fingertips, gently loosen the skin from the chicken breast by sliding your hand between the skin and flesh. Cream together 50 g/2 oz of the butter with the saffron threads, the lemon rind and half the parsley, until smooth. Push the butter under the skin. Spread over the breast and the top of the thighs with your fingers. Pull the neck skin to tighten the skin over the breast and tuck under the bird, then secure with a skewer or cocktail stick.

2 Heat the olive oil and remaining butter in a large heavy-based frying pan and cook the onions and garlic cloves for 5 minutes, or until the onions are soft. Stir in the cumin seeds, cinnamon, pine nuts and sultanas and cook for 2 minutes. Season to taste with salt and pepper and place in a roasting tin.

3 Place the chicken, breast-side down, on the base of the onions and roast in the preheated oven for 45 minutes. Reduce the oven temperature to 170°C/325°F/Gas Mark 3. Turn the chicken breast-side up and stir the onions. Continue roasting until the chicken is a deep golden yellow and the onions are crisp. Allow to rest for 10 minutes, then sprinkle with the remaining parsley. Before serving, garnish with a sprig of parsley and serve immediately with the onions and garlic.

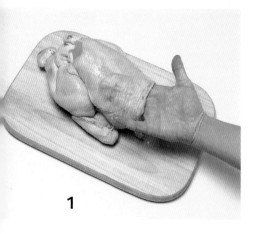

1

1

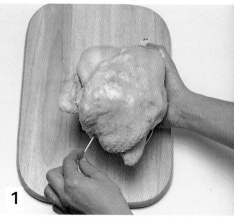

1

Pheasant with Portabella Mushrooms & Red Wine Gravy

INGREDIENTS

Serves 4

25 g/1 oz butter

1 tbsp olive oil

2 small pheasants (preferably hens)
  rinsed, well dried and halved

8 shallots, peeled

300 g/11 oz portabella mushrooms,
  thickly sliced

2–3 sprigs of fresh thyme or
  rosemary, leaves stripped

300 ml/½ pint Valpolicella or fruity
  red wine

300 ml/½ pint hot chicken stock

1 tbsp cornflour

2 tbsp balsamic vinegar

2 tbsp redcurrant jelly, or to taste

2 tbsp freshly chopped
  flat-leaf parsley

salt and freshly ground black pepper

sprigs of fresh thyme, to garnish

1 Preheat oven to 180°C/350°F/Gas Mark 4. Heat the butter and oil in a large saucepan or frying pan. Add the pheasant halves and shallots working in batches, if necessary, and cook for 10 minutes, or until golden on all sides, shaking the pan to glaze the shallots. Transfer to a casserole dish large enough to hold the pieces in a single layer. Add the mushroom and thyme to the pan and cook for 2–3 minutes, or until beginning to colour. Transfer to the dish with the pheasant halves.

2 Add the wine to the saucepan, it will bubble and steam. Cook, stirring up any browned bits from the pan and allow to reduce by half. Pour in the stock and bring to the boil, then pour over the pheasant halves. Cover and braise in the preheated oven for 50 minutes, or until tender. Remove the pheasant halves and vegetables to a wide, shallow serving dish and set the casserole or roasting tin over a medium-high heat.

3 Skim off any surface fat and bring to the boil. Blend the cornflour with the vinegar and stir into the sauce with the redcurrant jelly. Boil until the sauce is reduced and thickened slightly. Stir in the parsley and season to taste with salt and pepper. Pour over the pheasant halves, garnish with sprigs of fresh thyme and serve immediately.

1

1

3

Pheasant with Sage & Blueberries

INGREDIENTS

Serves 4

3 tbsp olive oil

3 shallots, peeled and
   coarsely chopped

2 sprigs of fresh sage,
   coarsely chopped

1 bay leaf

1 lemon, halved

salt and freshly ground
   black pepper

2 pheasants or guinea fowl,
   rinsed and dried

125 g/4 oz blueberries

4 slices Parma ham or bacon

125 ml/4 fl oz vermouth or dry
   white wine

200 ml/⅓ pint chicken stock

3 tbsp double cream or
   butter (optional)

1 tbsp brandy

roast potatoes, to serve

1. Preheat oven to 180°C/350°F/Gas Mark 4, 10 minutes before cooking. Place the oil, shallots, sage and bay leaf in a bowl, with the juice from the lemon halves. Season with salt and pepper. Tuck each of the squeezed lemon halves into the birds with 75 g/3 oz of the blueberries, then rub the birds with the marinade and leave for 2–3 hours, basting occasionally.

2. Remove the birds from the marinade and cover each with 2 slices of Parma ham. Tie the legs of each bird with string and place in a roasting tin. Pour over the marinade and add the vermouth. Roast in the preheated oven for 1 hour, or until tender and golden and the juices run clear when a thigh is pierced with a sharp knife or skewer.

3. Transfer to a warm serving plate, cover with tinfoil and discard the string. Skim off any surface fat from the tin and set over a medium-high heat.

4. Add the stock to the tin and bring to the boil, scraping any browned bits from the bottom. Boil until slightly reduced. Whisk in the cream or butter, if using, and simmer until thickened, whisking constantly. Stir in the brandy and strain into a gravy jug. Add the remaining blueberries and keep warm.

5. Using a sharp carving knife, cut each of the birds in half and arrange on the plate with the crispy Parma ham. Serve immediately with roast potatoes and the gravy.

1

2

5

Spatchcocked Poussins with Garlic Sage Butter

INGREDIENTS

Serves 4

For the herb butter:
6 large garlic cloves
150 g/5 oz butter, softened
2 tbsp freshly snipped chives
2 tbsp freshly chopped sage
grated rind and juice of 1 lemon
salt and ground black pepper

For the poussins:
4 spatchcocked poussins
2 tbsp extra virgin olive oil

To garnish:
chives
fresh sage leaves

To serve:
grilled quick-cook polenta
grilled tomatoes

1 Preheat grill and line the grill rack with tinfoil, before cooking. Put the garlic cloves in a small saucepan and cover with cold water. Bring to the boil, then simmer for 5 minutes, or until softened. Drain and cool slightly. Cut off the root end of each clove and squeeze the softened garlic into a bowl.

2 Pound the garlic until smooth, then beat in the butter, chives, sage and lemon rind and juice. Season to taste with salt and pepper.

3 Gently loosen the skin from each poussin breast by sliding your hand between the skin and the flesh. Push one-quarter of the herb butter under the skin, spreading evenly over the breast and the top of the thighs. Pull the neck skin gently to tighten the skin over the breast and tuck under the bird. Repeat with the remaining birds and herb butter.

4 Thread two wooden skewers crossways through each bird, from one wing through the opposite leg, to keep the poussin flat. Repeat with the remaining birds, brush with the olive oil and season with salt and pepper.

5 Arrange the poussins on the rack over the foil-lined rack and grill for 25 minutes, turning occasionally, until golden and crisp and the juices run clear when a thigh is pierced with a sharp knife or skewer. (Position the rack about 12.5 cm/5 inches from the heat source or the skin will brown before the birds are cooked through.) Garnish with chives and sage leaves and serve immediately with grilled polenta and a few grilled tomatoes.

2

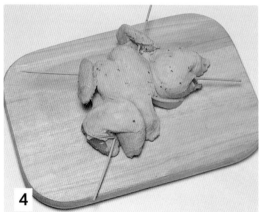

4

5

Chicken Cacciatore

INGREDIENTS

Serves 4

2–3 tbsp olive oil

125 g/4 oz pancetta or streaky
  bacon, diced

25 g/1 oz plain flour

salt and freshly ground black pepper

1.4–1.6 kg/3–3½ lb chicken, cut into
  8 pieces

2 garlic cloves, peeled and chopped

125 ml/4 fl oz red wine

400 g can chopped tomatoes

150 ml/¼ pint chicken stock

12 small onions, peeled

1 bay leaf

1 tsp brown sugar

1 tsp dried oregano

1 green pepper, deseeded
  and chopped

225 g/8 oz chestnut or field
  mushrooms, thickly sliced

2 tbsp freshly chopped parsley

freshly cooked tagliatelle, to serve

TASTY TIP

Use chestnut or field mushrooms
in this recipe because they have a
stronger flavour than button
mushrooms and will also help to
add colour to the sauce.

1 Heat 1 tablespoon of the olive oil in a large, deep frying pan and add the diced pancetta or bacon and stir-fry for 2–3 minutes, or until crisp and golden brown. Using a slotted spoon, transfer the pancetta or bacon to a plate and reserve.

2 Season the flour with salt and pepper, then use to coat the chicken. Heat the remaining oil in the pan and brown the chicken pieces on all sides for about 15 minutes. Remove from the pan and add to the bacon.

3 Stir the garlic into the pan and cook for about 30 seconds. Add the red wine and cook, stirring and scraping any browned bits from the base of the pan. Allow the wine to boil until it is reduced by half. Add the tomatoes, stock, onions, bay leaf, brown sugar and oregano and stir well. Season to taste.

4 Return the chicken and bacon to the pan and bring to the boil. Cover and simmer for 30 minutes, then stir in the peppers and mushrooms and simmer for a further 15–20 minutes, or until the chicken and vegetables are tender and the sauce is reduced and slightly thickened. Stir in the chopped parsley and serve immediately with freshly cooked tagliatelle.

2

3

4

Lemon Chicken with Potatoes, Rosemary & Olives

INGREDIENTS

Serves 6

12 skinless boneless chicken thighs
1 large lemon
125 ml/4 fl oz extra-virgin olive oil
6 garlic cloves, peeled and sliced
2 onions, peeled and thinly sliced
bunch of fresh rosemary
1.1 kg/2½ lb potatoes, peeled and cut
 into 4 cm/1½ inch pieces
salt and freshly ground black pepper
18–24 black olives, pitted

To serve:

steamed carrots
courgettes

HELPFUL HINT

It is worth seeking out unwaxed lemons for this recipe, or for any recipe in which the lemon zest is to be eaten. If unwaxed fruit are unavailable, pour hot water over them and scrub well before removing the zest.

1 Preheat oven to 200°C/400°F/Gas Mark 6, 15 minutes before cooking. Trim the chicken thighs and place in a shallow baking dish large enough to hold them in a single layer. Remove the rind from the lemon with a zester or if using a peeler cut into thin julienne strips. Reserve half and add the remainder to the chicken. Squeeze the lemon juice over the chicken, toss to coat well and leave to stand for 10 minutes.

2 Transfer the chicken to a roasting tin. Add the remaining lemon zest or julienne strips, olive oil, garlic, onions and half of the rosemary sprigs. Toss gently and leave for about 20 minutes.

3 Cover the potatoes with lightly salted water and bring to the boil. Cook for 2 minutes, then drain well and add to the chicken. Season to taste with salt and pepper.

4 Roast the chicken in the preheated oven for 50 minutes, turning frequently and basting, or until the chicken is cooked. Just before the end of cooking time, discard the rosemary, and add fresh sprigs of rosemary. Add the olives and stir. Serve immediately with steamed carrots and courgettes.

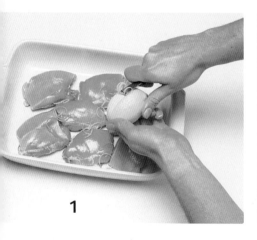
1

2

4

Chicken with Porcini Mushrooms & Cream

INGREDIENTS

Serves 4

2 tbsp olive oil

4 boneless chicken breasts,
preferably free range

2 garlic cloves, peeled and crushed

150 ml/¼ pint dry vermouth or dry
white wine

salt and freshly ground black pepper

25 g/1 oz butter

450 g/1 lb porcini or wild
mushrooms, thickly sliced

1 tbsp freshly chopped oregano

sprigs of fresh basil, to
garnish (optional)

freshly cooked rice, to serve

1 Heat the olive oil in a large, heavy-based frying pan, then add the chicken breasts, skin-side down and cook for about 10 minutes, or until they are well browned. Remove the chicken breasts and reserve. Add the garlic, stir into the juices and cook for 1 minute.

2 Pour the vermouth or white wine into the pan and season to taste with salt and pepper. Return the chicken to the pan. Bring to the boil, reduce the heat to low and simmer for about 20 minutes, or until tender.

3 In another large frying pan, heat the butter and add the sliced porcini or wild mushrooms. Stir-fry for about 5 minutes, or until the mushrooms are golden and tender.

4 Add the porcini or wild mushrooms and any juices to the chicken. Season to taste, then add the chopped oregano. Stir together gently and cook for 1 minute longer. Transfer to a large serving plate and garnish with sprigs of fresh basil, if desired. Serve immediately with rice.

TASTY TIP

Porcini or cep mushrooms grow wild and are relatively easy to find, if you know where to look. They can, however, be very expensive to buy fresh. If they are unavailable, substitute with fresh button or chestnut mushrooms and 15 g/½ oz reconstituted dried porcini instead.

2

3

4

Turkey Escalopes Marsala with Wilted Watercress

INGREDIENTS

Serves 4

4 turkey escalopes, each about
  150 g/5 oz
25 g/1 oz plain flour
$1/2$ tsp dried thyme
salt and freshly ground black pepper
1–2 tbsp olive oil
125 g/4 oz watercress
40 g/$1^1/2$ oz butter
225 g/8 oz mushrooms, wiped
  and quartered
50 ml/2 fl oz dry Marsala wine
50 ml/2 fl oz chicken stock or water

HELPFUL HINT

Turkey escalopes are simply thin slices of turkey breast fillets which have been flattened. If they are unavailable, substitute chicken breasts that have been halved horizontally and flattened between pieces of clingfilm.

1 Place each turkey escalope between 2 sheets of non-stick baking parchment and using a meat mallet or rolling pin pound to make an escalope about 3 mm/$1/8$ inch thick. Put the flour in a shallow dish, add the thyme, season to taste with salt and pepper and stir to blend. Coat each escalope lightly on both sides with the flour mixture, then reserve.

2 Heat the olive oil in a large frying pan, then add the watercress and stir-fry for about 2 minutes, until just wilted and brightly coloured. Season with salt and pepper. Using a slotted spoon, transfer the watercress to a plate and keep warm.

3 Add half the butter to the frying pan and when melted, add the mushrooms. Stir-fry for 4 minutes, or until golden and tender. Remove from the pan and reserve.

4 Add the remaining butter to the pan and, working in batches if necessary, cook the flour-coated escalopes for 2–3 minutes on each side, or until golden and cooked thoroughly, adding the remaining oil, if necessary. Remove from the pan and keep warm.

5 Add the Marsala wine to the pan and stir, scraping up any browned bits from the bottom of the pan. Add the stock or water and bring to the boil over a high heat. Season lightly.

6 Return the escalopes and mushrooms to the pan and reheat gently until piping hot. Divide the warm watercress between 4 serving plates.

7 Arrange 1 escalope over each serving of wilted watercress and spoon over the mushrooms and Marsala sauce. Serve immediately.

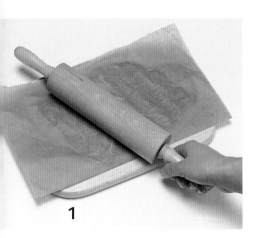

1

2

4

Lemon Chicken with Basil & Linguine

INGREDIENTS

Serves 4

grated rind and juice of 1 large lemon

2 garlic cloves, peeled and crushed

2 tbsp basil-flavoured extra-virgin
olive oil

4 tbsp freshly chopped basil

salt and freshly ground black pepper

450 g/1 lb skinless, boneless chicken
breast, cut into bite-sized pieces

1 onion, peeled and finely chopped

3 celery stalks, trimmed and
thinly sliced

175 g/6 oz mushrooms, wiped
and halved

2 tbsp plain flour

150 ml/¼ pint white wine

150 ml/¼ pint chicken stock

350–450 g/12 oz–1 lb linguine

To garnish:

lemon zest

fresh basil leaves

1 Blend the lemon rind and juice, garlic, half the oil, half the basil and salt and pepper in a large bowl. Add the chicken pieces and toss well to coat. Allow to stand for about 1 hour, stirring occasionally.

2 Heat the remaining oil in a large non-stick frying pan, then add the sliced onion and cook for 3–4 minutes, or until slightly softened. Using a slotted spoon, drain the chicken pieces and add to the frying pan, reserving the marinade. Cook the chicken for 2–3 minutes, or until golden brown, then add the sliced celery and mushroom halves and cook for a further 2–3 minutes.

3 Sprinkle in the flour and stir until the chicken and vegetables are coated. Gradually stir the wine into the pan until a thick sauce forms, then stir in the stock and reserved marinade. Bring to the boil, stirring constantly. Cover and simmer for about 10 minutes, then stir in the remaining basil.

4 Meanwhile, bring a large saucepan of lightly salted water to the boil. Slowly add the linguine and simmer for 7–10 minutes, or until 'al dente'. Drain well and turn into a large serving bowl, pour over the sauce and garnish with the lemon zest and fresh basil leaves. Serve immediately.

1

2

3

Chicken Liver &
Tomato Sauce with Tagliolini

INGREDIENTS

Serves 4

50 ml/2 fl oz extra-virgin olive oil

1 onion, peeled and finely chopped

2 garlic cloves, peeled and
finely chopped

125 ml/4 fl oz dry red wine

2 x 400 g cans Italian peeled plum
tomatoes with juice

1 tbsp tomato purée

1 tbsp freshly chopped sage or
thyme leaves

salt and freshly ground black pepper

350 g/12 oz fresh or dried tagliolini,
papardelle or tagliatelle

25 g/1 oz butter

225 g/8 oz fresh chicken livers,
trimmed and cut in half

plain flour for dusting

sprigs of fresh sage, to
garnish (optional)

1   Heat half the olive oil in a large, deep, heavy-based frying pan and add the onion. Cook, stirring frequently, for 4–5 minutes, or until soft and translucent. Stir in the garlic and cook for a further minute.

2   Add the red wine and cook, stirring until the wine is reduced by half, then add the tomatoes, tomato purée and half the sage or thyme. Bring to the boil, stirring to break up the tomatoes. Simmer for 30 minutes, stirring occasionally, or until the sauce has reduced and thickened. Season to taste with salt and pepper.

3   Bring a large saucepan of lightly salted water to the boil. Add the pasta and cook for 7–10 minutes, or until 'al dente'.

4   Meanwhile, in a large heavy-based frying pan, melt the remaining oil and the butter and heat until very hot. Pat the chicken livers dry and dust lightly with a little flour. Add to the pan, a few at a time, and cook for 5 minutes, or until crisp and browned, turning carefully – the livers should still be pink inside.

5   Drain the pasta well and turn into a large, warmed serving bowl. Stir the livers carefully into the tomato sauce, then pour the sauce over the drained pasta and toss gently to coat. Garnish with a sprig of fresh sage and serve immediately.

2

2

4

Creamy Chicken Cannelloni

INGREDIENTS

Serves 6

50 g/2 oz butter

2 garlic cloves, peeled and
finely crushed

225 g/8 oz button mushrooms,
thinly sliced

2 tbsp freshly chopped basil

450 g/1 lb fresh spinach, blanched

salt and freshly ground black pepper

2 tbsp plain flour

300 ml/½ pint chicken stock

150 ml/¼ pint dry white wine

150 ml/¼ pint double cream

350 g/12 oz skinless, boneless,
cooked chicken, chopped

175 g/6 oz Parma ham,
finely chopped

½ tsp dried thyme

225 g/8 oz precooked
cannelloni tubes

175 g/6 oz Gruyère cheese, grated

40 g/1 ½ oz Parmesan cheese, grated

sprig of fresh basil, to garnish

1 Preheat oven to 190°C/375°F/Gas Mark 5, 10 minutes before cooking. Lightly butter a 28 x 23 cm/11 x 9 inch ovenproof baking dish. Heat half the butter in a large heavy-based frying pan, then add the garlic and mushrooms and cook gently for 5 minutes. Stir in the basil and the spinach and cook, covered, until the spinach is wilted and just tender, stirring frequently. Season to taste with salt and pepper, then spoon into the dish and reserve.

2 Melt the remaining butter in a small saucepan, then stir in the flour and cook for about 2 minutes, stirring constantly. Remove from the heat, stir in the stock, then the wine and the cream. Return to the heat, bring to the boil and simmer, until the sauce is thick and smooth, then season to taste.

3 Measure 125 ml/4 fl oz of the cream sauce into a bowl. Add the chopped chicken, Parma ham and the dried thyme. Season to taste, then spoon the chicken mixture into the cannelloni tubes, arranging them in 2 long rows on top of the spinach layer.

4 Add half the Gruyère cheese to the cream sauce and heat, stirring, until the cheese melts. Pour over the sauce and top with the remaining Gruyère and the Parmesan cheeses. Bake in the preheated oven for 35 minutes, or until golden and bubbling. Garnish with a sprig of fresh basil and serve immediately.

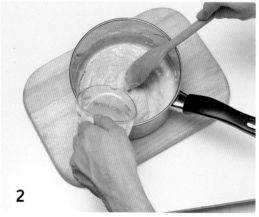

1

2

3

Duck Lasagna with Porcini & Basil

INGREDIENTS

Serves 6

1.4–1.8 kg/3–4 lb duck, quartered

1 onion, unpeeled and quartered

2 carrots, peeled and cut into pieces

1 celery stalk, cut into pieces

1 leek, trimmed and cut into pieces

2 garlic cloves, unpeeled
  and smashed

1 tbsp black peppercorns

2 bay leaves

6–8 sprigs of fresh thyme

50 g/2 oz dried porcini mushrooms

125 ml/4 oz dry sherry

75 g/3 oz butter, diced

1 bunch of fresh basil leaves, stripped
  from stems

24 precooked lasagna sheets

75 g/3 oz Parmesan cheese, grated

sprig of parsley, to garnish

mixed salad, to serve

1 Preheat oven to 180°C/350°F/Gas Mark 4, 10 minutes before cooking. Put the duck with the vegetables, garlic, peppercorns, bay leaves and thyme into a large stock pot and cover with cold water. Bring to the boil, skimming off any fat, then reduce the heat and simmer for 1 hour. Transfer the duck to a bowl and cool slightly.

2 When cool enough to handle, remove the meat from the duck and dice. Return all the bones and trimmings to the simmering stock and continue to simmer for 1 hour. Strain the stock into a large bowl and leave until cold. Remove and discard the fat that has risen to the top of the stock.

3 Put the porcini in a colander and rinse under cold running water. Leave for 1 minute to dry off, then turn out on to a chopping board and chop finely. Place in a small bowl, then pour over the sherry and leave for about 1 hour, or until the porcini are plump and all the sherry is absorbed.

4 Heat 25 g/1 oz of the butter in a frying pan. Shred the basil leaves and add to the hot butter, stirring until wilted. Add the soaked porcini and any liquid, mix well and reserve.

5 Oil a 30.5 x 23 cm/12 x 9 inch deep baking dish and pour a little stock into the base. Cover with 6–8 lasagna sheets, making sure that sheets slightly overlap. Continue to layer the pasta with a little stock, duck meat, the mushroom-basil mixture and Parmesan. Add a little butter every other layer.

6 Cover with tinfoil and bake in the preheated oven for 40–45 minutes, or until cooked. Stand for 10 minutes before serving. Garnish with a sprig of parsley and serve with salad.

1

2

3

Turkey Tetrazzini

INGREDIENTS

Serves 4

275 g/10 oz green and
   white tagliatelle
50 g/2 oz butter
4 slices streaky bacon, diced
1 onion, peeled and finely chopped
175 g/6 oz mushrooms, thinly sliced
40 g/1½ oz plain flour
450 ml/¾ pint chicken stock
150 ml/¼ pint double cream
2 tbsp sherry
450 g/1 lb cooked turkey meat, cut
   into bite-sized pieces
1 tbsp freshly chopped parsley
freshly grated nutmeg
salt and freshly ground black pepper
25 g/1 oz Parmesan cheese, grated

To garnish:
freshly chopped parsley
Parmesan cheese, grated

TASTY TIP
This is a great way to use Christmas leftovers – it is worth putting extra meat in the freezer. Use frozen leftovers within 1 month.

1 Preheat oven to 180°C/350°F/Gas Mark 4. Lightly oil a large ovenproof dish. Bring a large saucepan of lightly salted water to the boil. Add the tagliatelle and cook for 7–9 minutes, or until 'al dente'. Drain well and reserve.

2 In a heavy-based saucepan, heat the butter and add the bacon. Cook for 2–3 minutes, or until crisp and golden. Add the onion and mushrooms and cook for 3–4 minutes, or until the vegetables are tender.

3 Stir in the flour and cook for 2 minutes. Remove from the heat and slowly stir in the stock. Return to the heat and cook, stirring until a smooth, thick sauce has formed. Add the tagliatelle, then pour in the cream and sherry. Add the turkey and parsley. Season to taste with the nutmeg and salt and pepper. Toss well to coat.

4 Turn the mixture into the prepared dish, spreading evenly. Sprinkle the top with the Parmesan cheese and bake in the preheated oven for 30–35 minutes, or until crisp, golden and bubbling. Garnish with chopped parsley and Parmesan cheese. Serve straight from the dish.

Poached Chicken with Salsa Verde Herb Sauce

INGREDIENTS

Serves 6

6 boneless chicken breasts, each
    about 175 g/6 oz
600 ml/1 pint chicken stock,
    preferably homemade

For the salsa verde:

2 garlic cloves, peeled and chopped
4 tbsp freshly chopped parsley
3 tbsp freshly chopped mint
2 tsp capers
2 tbsp chopped gherkins (optional)
2–3 anchovy fillets in olive oil,
    drained and finely chopped
    (optional)
1 handful wild rocket leaves,
    chopped (optional)
2 tbsp lemon juice or red
    wine vinegar
125 ml/4 fl oz extra-virgin
    olive oil
salt and freshly ground black pepper
sprigs of mint, to garnish
freshly cooked vegetables, to serve

1 Place the chicken breasts with the stock in a large frying pan and bring to the boil. Reduce the heat and simmer for 10–15 minutes, or until cooked. Leave to cool in the stock.

2 To make the salsa verde, switch the motor on a food processor, then drop in the garlic cloves and chop finely. Add the parsley and mint and, using the pulse button, pulse 2–3 times. Add the capers and, if using, add the gherkins, anchovies and rocket. Pulse 2–3 times until the sauce is evenly textured.

3 With the machine still running, pour in the lemon juice or red wine vinegar, then add the olive oil in a slow, steady stream until the sauce is smooth. Season to taste with salt and pepper, then transfer to a large serving bowl and reserve.

4 Carve each chicken breast into thick slices and arrange on serving plates, fanning out the slices slightly. Spoon over a little of the salsa verde on to each chicken breast, garnish with sprigs of mint and serve immediately with freshly cooked vegetables.

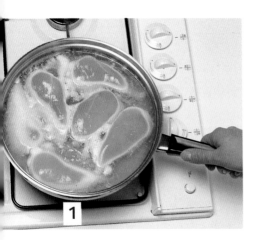

1

3

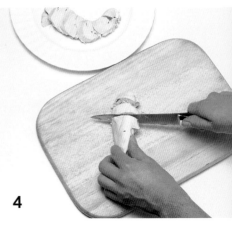

4

Chicken Parcels with Courgettes & Pasta

INGREDIENTS

Serves 4

2 tbsp olive oil

125 g/4 oz farfalle pasta

1 onion, peeled and thinly sliced

1 garlic clove, peeled and finely
    chopped

2 medium courgettes, trimmed and
    thinly sliced

salt and freshly ground black pepper

2 tbsp freshly chopped oregano

4 plum tomatoes, deseeded and
    coarsely chopped

4 x 175 g/6 oz boneless, skinless
    chicken breasts

150 ml/¼ pint Italian white wine

1 Preheat oven to 200°C/400°F/Gas Mark 6, 15 minutes before cooking. Lightly brush 4 large sheets of non-stick baking parchment with half the oil. Bring a saucepan of lightly salted water to the boil and cook the pasta for 10 minutes, or until 'al dente'. Drain and reserve.

2 Heat the remaining oil in a frying pan and cook the onion for 2–3 minutes. Add the garlic and cook for 1 minute. Add the courgettes and cook for 1 minute, then remove from the heat, season to taste with salt and pepper and add half the oregano.

3 Divide the cooked pasta equally between the 4 sheets of baking parchment, positioning the pasta in the centre. Top the pasta with equal amounts of the vegetable mixture, and sprinkle a quarter of the chopped tomatoes over each.

4 Score the surface of each chicken breast about 1 cm/½ inch deep. Place a chicken breast on top of the pasta and sprinkle each with the remaining oregano and the white wine. Fold the edges of the paper along the top, then along each side, creating a sealed envelope.

5 Bake in the preheated oven for 30–35 minutes, or until cooked. Serve immediately.

HELPFUL HINT

This is a great recipe for entertaining. The parcels can be prepared ahead and baked when needed. For a dramatic presentation, serve in the paper.

2

3

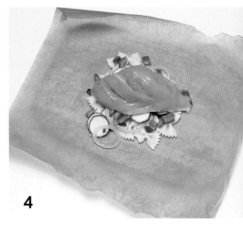

4

Chicken Under a Brick

INGREDIENTS

Serves 4

1.8 kg/4 lb free range corn-fed,
    oven-ready chicken
50 ml/2 fl oz olive oil
sea salt and freshly ground black
    pepper

To garnish:

sprigs of fresh basil
chives
tossed bitter salad leaves, to serve

TASTY TIP

In a large bowl, whisk together
1 teaspoon of whole-grain
mustard, 1 crushed garlic clove,
2 teaspoons of balsamic vinegar
and seasoning. When combined
thoroughly, whisk in 3–4
tablespoons of good-quality olive
oil to taste. Toss with a mixture of
bitter leaves such as frisée,
radicchio, and chicory and serve
with the chicken.

1 Rinse the chicken and dry well, inside and out. Using poultry shears or kitchen scissors, cut along each side of the backbone of the chicken and discard or use for stock. Place the chicken skin-side up on a work surface and, using the palm of your hand, press down firmly to break the breast bone and flatten the bird.

2 Turn the chicken breast-side up and use a sharp knife to slit the skin between the breast and thigh on each side. Fold the legs in and push the drumstick bones through the slits. Tuck the wing under, the chicken should be as flat as possible.

3 Heat the olive oil in a large, heavy-based frying pan until very hot, but not smoking. Place the chicken in the pan, skin-side down, and place a flat lid or plate directly on top of the chicken. Top with a brick (hence the name) or 2 kg/5 lb weight. Cook for 12–15 minutes, or until golden brown.

4 Remove the weights and lid and, using a pair of tongs, turn the chicken carefully, then season to taste with salt and pepper. Cover and weight the lid again, then cook for 12–15 minutes longer, until the chicken is tender and the juices run clear when a thigh is pierced with a sharp knife or skewer.

5 Transfer the chicken to a serving plate and cover loosely with tinfoil to keep warm. Allow to rest for at least 10 minutes before carving. Garnish with sprigs of basil and chives and serve with salad leaves.

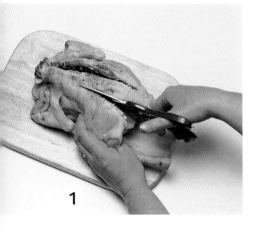

1

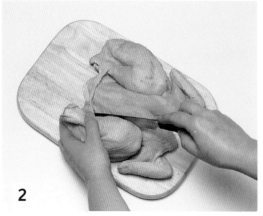

2

3

Chicken & Asparagus with Tagliatelle

INGREDIENTS

Serves 4

275 g/10 oz fresh asparagus

50 g/2 oz butter

4 spring onions, trimmed and
  coarsely chopped

350 g/12 oz boneless, skinless
  chicken breast, thinly sliced

2 tbsp white vermouth

300 ml/½ pint double cream

2 tbsp freshly chopped chives

400 g/14 oz fresh tagliatelle

50 g/2 oz Parmesan or pecorino
  cheese, grated

snipped chives, to garnish

extra Parmesan cheese (optional),
  to serve

1   Using a swivel-bladed vegetable peeler, lightly peel the asparagus stalks and then cook in lightly salted, boiling water for 2–3 minutes, or until just tender. Drain and refresh in cold water, then cut into 4 cm/1½ inch pieces and reserve.

2   Melt the butter in a large frying pan then add the spring onions and the chicken and fry for 4 minutes. Add the vermouth and allow to reduce until the liquid has evaporated. Pour in the cream and half the chives. Cook gently for 5–7 minutes, until the sauce has thickened and slightly reduced and the chicken is tender.

3   Bring a large saucepan of lightly salted water to the boil and cook the tagliatelle for 4–5 minutes, or until 'al dente'. Drain and add immediately to the chicken and cream sauce.

4   Using a pair of spaghetti tongs or kitchen forks, lightly toss the sauce and pasta until it is mixed thoroughly. Add the remaining chives and the Parmesan cheese and toss gently. Garnish with snipped chives and serve immediately, with extra Parmesan cheese, if you like.

TASTY TIP

Freshly made pasta will cook in 30–60 seconds. It is cooked when it rises to the surface. Bought fresh pasta will take between 2–3 minutes. Dried pasta takes longer to cook (between 4–10 minutes) depending on the variety – check the packet instructions.

Marinated Pheasant Breasts with Grilled Polenta

INGREDIENTS

Serves 4

3 tbsp extra-virgin olive oil
1 tbsp freshly chopped rosemary
  or sage leaves
½ tsp ground cinnamon
grated zest of 1 orange
salt and freshly ground black pepper
8 pheasant or wood pigeon breasts
600 ml/1 pint water
125 g/4 oz quick-cook polenta
2 tbsp butter, diced
40 g/1½ oz Parmesan cheese, grated
1–2 tbsp freshly chopped parsley
assorted salad leaves, to serve

TASTY TIP

Heat a griddle pan and griddle the pigeon breasts, skin-side down for 2–3 minutes. Turn and griddle 2 minutes longer for rare, 3–4 minutes longer if you prefer them well done.

1 Preheat grill just before cooking. Blend 2 tablespoons of the olive oil with the chopped rosemary or sage, cinnamon and orange zest and season to taste with salt and pepper.

2 Place the pheasant breasts in a large, shallow dish, pour over the oil and marinate until required, turning occasionally.

3 Bring the water and 1 teaspoon of salt to the boil in a large, heavy-based saucepan. Slowly whisk in the polenta in a thin, steady stream. Reduce the heat and simmer for 5–10 minutes, or until very thick, stirring constantly.

4 Stir the butter and cheese into the polenta, the parsley and a little black pepper.

5 Turn the polenta out on to a lightly oiled, non-stick baking tray and spread into an even layer about 2 cm/¾ inch thick. Leave to cool, then chill in the refrigerator for about 1 hour, or until the polenta is chilled.

6 Turn the cold polenta on to a work surface. Cut into 10 cm/4 inch squares. Brush with olive oil and arrange on a grill rack. Grill for 2–3 minutes on each side until crisp and golden, then cut each square into triangles and keep warm.

7 Transfer the marinated pheasant breasts to the grill rack and grill for 5 minutes, or until crisp and beginning to colour, turning once. Serve the pheasants immediately with the polenta triangles and salad leaves.

3

4

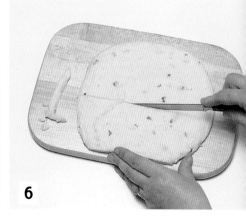

6

Braised Rabbit with Red Peppers

INGREDIENTS

Serves 4

1.1 kg/2½ lb rabbit pieces
125 ml/4 fl oz olive oil
grated zest and juice of 1 lemon
2–3 tbsp freshly chopped thyme
salt and freshly ground black pepper
1 onion, peeled and thinly sliced
4 red peppers, deseeded and cut into
  2.5 cm/1 inch pieces
2 garlic cloves, peeled and crushed
400 g can strained, crushed
  tomatoes
1 tsp brown sugar
freshly cooked polenta or creamy
  mashed potatoes, to serve

1 Place the rabbit pieces in a shallow dish with half the olive oil, the lemon zest and juice, thyme, and some black pepper. Turn until well coated, then cover and leave to marinate for about 1 hour.

2 Heat half the remaining oil in a large, heavy-based casserole dish, add the onion and cook for 5 minutes, then add the peppers and cook for a further 12–15 minutes, or until softened, stirring occasionally. Stir in the garlic, crushed tomatoes and brown sugar and cook, covered, until soft, stirring occasionally.

3 Heat the remaining oil in a large frying pan, drain the rabbit, reserving the marinade, and pat the rabbit dry with absorbent kitchen paper. Add the rabbit to the pan and cook on all sides until golden. Transfer the rabbit to the casserole dish and mix to cover with the tomato sauce.

4 Add the reserved marinade to the frying pan, and cook, stirring to loosen any browned bits from the pan. Add to the rabbit and stir gently.

5 Cover the pan and simmer for 30 minutes or until the rabbit is tender. Serve the rabbit and the vegetable mixture on a bed of polenta or creamy mashed potatoes.

HELPFUL HINT

Casseroling is an excellent way to cook rabbit as it has a tendency to be dry. Buy from a good-quality butcher, who will also be able to joint it for you.

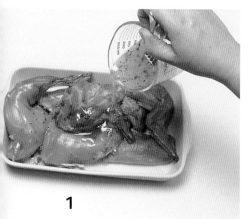
1

3

4

Chicken & Pasta Salad

INGREDIENTS

Serves 4

450 g/1 lb short pasta

2–3 tbsp extra-virgin olive oil

300 g/11 oz cold cooked chicken
  (preferably roasted), cut into
  bite-sized pieces

1 red pepper, deseeded and diced

1 yellow pepper, deseeded and diced

4–5 sun-dried tomatoes, sliced

2 tbsp capers, rinsed and drained

125 g/4 oz pitted Italian black olives

4 spring onions, chopped

225 g/8 oz mozzarella cheese,
  preferably buffalo, diced

salt and freshly ground black pepper

For the dressing:

50 ml/2 fl oz red or white
  wine vinegar

1 tbsp mild mustard

1 tsp sugar

75–125 ml/ 3–4 fl oz extra-virgin
  olive oil

125 ml/4 fl oz mayonnaise

1 Bring a large saucepan of lightly salted water to the boil.
Add the pasta and cook for 10 minutes, or until 'al dente'.

2 Drain the pasta and rinse under cold running water, then drain
again. Place in a large serving bowl and toss with the olive oil.

3 Add the chicken, diced red and yellow peppers, sliced sun-dried
tomatoes, capers, olives, spring onions and mozzarella to the pasta
and toss gently until mixed. Season to taste with salt and pepper.

4 To make the dressing, put the vinegar, mustard and sugar into a
small bowl or jug and whisk until well blended and the sugar is
dissolved. Season with some pepper, then gradually whisk in the
olive oil in a slow, steady stream until a thickened vinaigrette forms.

5 Put the mayonnaise in a bowl and gradually whisk in the dressing
until smooth. Pour over the pasta mixture and mix gently until all
the ingredients are coated. Turn into a large, shallow serving bowl
and serve at room temperature.

3

4

4

Risi e Bisi

INGREDIENTS

Serves 4

700 g/1½ lb young peas in pods
   or 175 g/6 oz frozen petits
   pois, thawed
25 g/1 oz unsalted butter
1 tsp olive oil
3 rashers pancetta or unsmoked
   back bacon, chopped
1 small onion, peeled and
   finely chopped
1 garlic clove, peeled and
   finely chopped
1.3 litres/2¼ pints vegetable stock
pinch of caster sugar
1 tsp lemon juice
1 bay leaf
200 g/7 oz Arborio rice
3 tbsp freshly chopped parsley
50 g/2 oz Parmesan cheese,
   finely grated
salt and freshly ground black pepper

To garnish:
sprig of fresh parsley
julienne strips of orange rind

1 Shell the peas, if using fresh ones. Melt the butter and olive oil together in a large, heavy-based saucepan. Add the chopped pancetta or bacon, the chopped onion and garlic and gently fry for about 10 minutes, or until the onion is softened and is just beginning to colour.

2 Pour in the vegetable stock, then add the caster sugar, lemon juice and bay leaf. Add the fresh peas if using. Bring the mixture to a fast boil.

3 Add the rice, stir and simmer, uncovered, for about 20 minutes, or until the rice is tender. Occasionally, stir the mixture gently while it cooks. If using frozen petits pois, stir them into the rice about 2 minutes before the end of the cooking time.

4 When the rice is cooked, remove the bay leaf and discard. Stir in 2½ tablespoons of the chopped parsley and the grated Parmesan cheese. Season to taste with salt and pepper.

5 Transfer the rice to a large serving dish. Garnish with the remaining chopped parsley, a sprig of fresh parsley and julienne strips of orange rind. Serve immediately while piping hot.

1

2

4

Rice & Vegetable Timbale

INGREDIENTS

Serves 6

25 g/1 oz dried white breadcrumbs
3 tbsp olive oil
2 courgettes, sliced
1 small aubergine, cut into
   1 cm/½ inch dice
175 g/6 oz mushrooms, sliced
1 garlic clove, peeled and crushed
1 tsp balsamic vinegar
1 onion, peeled and finely chopped
25 g/1 oz unsalted butter
400 g/14 oz Arborio rice
about 1.3 litres/2¼ pints boiling
   vegetable stock
2 medium eggs, lightly beaten
25 g/1 oz Parmesan cheese,
   finely grated
2 tbsp freshly chopped basil
salt and freshly ground black pepper

To garnish:

sprig of fresh basil
1 radish, thinly sliced

1 Preheat oven to 190°C/375°F/Gas Mark 5, 10 minutes before cooking. Sprinkle the breadcrumbs over the base and sides of a thickly buttered 20.5 cm/8 inch round loose-bottomed tin.

2 Heat the olive oil in a large frying pan and gently fry the courgettes, aubergine, mushrooms and garlic for 5 minutes, or until beginning to soften. Stir in the vinegar. Tip the vegetables into a large sieve placed over a bowl to catch the juices.

3 Fry the onion gently in the butter for 10 minutes, until soft. Add the rice and stir for a minute to coat. Add a ladleful of stock and any juices from the vegetables and simmer, stirring, until the rice has absorbed all of the liquid.

4 Continue adding the stock in this way, until the rice is just tender. This should take about 20 minutes. Remove from the heat and leave to cool for 5 minutes. Stir in the eggs, cheese and basil. Season to taste with salt and pepper.

5 Spoon a quarter of the rice into the prepared tin. Top with one-third of the vegetable mixture. Continue layering up in this way, finishing with a layer of rice.

6 Level the top of the layer of rice, gently pressing down the mixture. Cover with a piece of tinfoil. Put on a baking sheet and bake in the preheated oven for 50 minutes, or until firm.

7 Leave the timbale to stand in the tin for 10 minutes, still covered with tinfoil, then turn out on to a warmed serving platter. Garnish with a sprig of fresh basil and slices of radish and serve immediately.

1

2

5

Vegetables Braised in Olive Oil & Lemon

INGREDIENTS

Serves 4

small strip of pared rind and juice
of ½ lemon
4 tbsp olive oil
1 bay leaf
large sprig of thyme
150 ml/¼ pint water
4 spring onions, trimmed and
finely chopped
175 g/6 oz baby button mushrooms
175 g/6 oz broccoli, cut into
small florets
175 g/6 oz cauliflower, cut into
small florets
1 medium courgette, sliced on
the diagonal
2 tbsp freshly snipped chives
salt and freshly ground black pepper
lemon zest, to garnish

TASTY TIP

Serve these vegetables as an accompaniment to roasted or grilled chicken, fish or turkey. Alternatively, toast some crusty bread, rub with a garlic clove and drizzle with a little olive oil and top with a spoonful of vegetables.

1 Put the pared lemon rind and juice into a large saucepan. Add the olive oil, bay leaf, thyme and the water. Bring to the boil. Add the spring onions and mushrooms. Top with the broccoli and cauliflower, trying to add them so that the stalks are submerged in the water and the tops are just above it. Cover and simmer for 3 minutes.

2 Scatter the courgettes on top, so that they are steamed rather than boiled. Cook, covered, for a further 3–4 minutes, until all the vegetables are tender. Using a slotted spoon, transfer the vegetables from the liquid into a warmed serving dish. Increase the heat and boil rapidly for 3–4 minutes, or until the liquid is reduced to about 8 tablespoons. Remove the lemon rind, bay leaf and thyme sprig and discard.

3 Stir the chives into the reduced liquid, season to taste with salt and pepper and pour over the vegetables. Sprinkle with lemon zest and serve immediately.

Melanzane Parmigiana

INGREDIENTS

Serves 4

900 g/2 lb aubergines
salt and freshly ground black pepper
5 tbsp olive oil
1 red onion, peeled and chopped
½ tsp mild paprika pepper
150 ml/¼ pint dry red wine
150 ml/¼ pint vegetable stock
400 g can chopped tomatoes
1 tsp tomato purée
1 tbsp freshly chopped oregano
175 g/6 oz mozzarella cheese,
   thinly sliced
40 g/1½ oz Parmesan cheese,
   coarsely grated
sprig of fresh basil, to garnish

1 Preheat oven to 200°C/400°F/Gas Mark 6, 15 minutes before cooking. Cut the aubergines lengthways into thin slices. Sprinkle with salt and leave to drain in a colander over a bowl for 30 minutes.

2 Meanwhile, heat 1 tablespoon of the olive oil in a saucepan and fry the onion for 10 minutes, until softened. Add the paprika and cook for 1 minute. Stir in the wine, stock, tomatoes and tomato purée. Simmer, uncovered, for 25 minutes, or until fairly thick. Stir in the oregano and season to taste with salt and pepper. Remove from the heat.

3 Rinse the aubergine slices thoroughly under cold water and pat dry on absorbent kitchen paper. Heat 2 tablespoons of the oil in a griddle pan and cook the aubergines in batches, for 3 minutes on each side, until golden. Drain well on absorbent kitchen paper.

4 Pour half of the tomato sauce into the base of a large ovenproof dish. Cover with half the aubergine slices, then top with the mozzarella. Cover with the remaining aubergine slices and pour over the remaining tomato sauce. Sprinkle with the grated Parmesan cheese.

5 Bake in the preheated oven for 30 minutes, or until the aubergines are tender and the sauce is bubbling. Garnish with a sprig of fresh basil and cool for a few minutes before serving.

HELPFUL HINT

Salting the aubergine draws out some of the moisture, so you'll need less oil when frying.

1

3

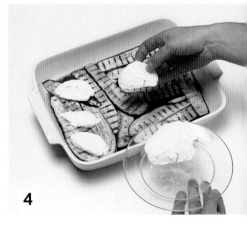
4

Stuffed Tomatoes with Grilled Polenta

INGREDIENTS

Serves 4

For the polenta:
300 ml/½ pint vegetable stock
salt and freshly ground black pepper
50 g/2 oz quick-cook polenta
15 g/½ oz butter

For the stuffed tomatoes:
4 large tomatoes
1 tbsp olive oil
1 garlic clove, peeled and crushed
1 bunch spring onions, trimmed and
  finely chopped
2 tbsp freshly chopped parsley
2 tbsp freshly chopped basil
2 slices Parma ham, cut into
  thin slivers
50 g/2 oz fresh white breadcrumbs
snipped chives, to garnish

1   Preheat grill just before cooking. To make the polenta, pour the stock into a saucepan. Add a pinch of salt and bring to the boil. Pour in the polenta in a fine stream, stirring all the time. Simmer for about 15 minutes, or until very thick. Stir in the butter and add a little pepper. Turn the polenta out on to a chopping board and spread to a thickness of just over 1 cm/½ inch. Cool, cover with clingfilm and chill in the refrigerator for 30 minutes.

2   To make the stuffed tomatoes, cut the tomatoes in half, then scoop out the seeds and press through a fine sieve to extract the juices. Season the insides of the tomatoes with salt and pepper and reserve.

3   Heat the olive oil in a saucepan and gently fry the garlic and spring onions for 3 minutes. Add the tomatoes' juices, bubble for 3–4 minutes, until most of the liquid has evaporated. Stir in the herbs, Parma ham and a little black pepper with half the breadcrumbs. Spoon into the hollowed out tomatoes and reserve.

4   Cut the polenta into 5 cm/2 inch squares, then cut each in half diagonally to make triangles. Put the triangles on a piece of tinfoil on the grill rack and grill for 4–5 minutes on each side, until golden. Cover and keep warm.

5   Grill the tomatoes under a medium-hot grill for about 4 minutes – any exposed Parma ham will become crisp. Sprinkle with the remaining breadcrumbs and grill for 1–2 minutes, or until the breadcrumbs are golden brown. Garnish with snipped chives and serve immediately with the grilled polenta.

1

3

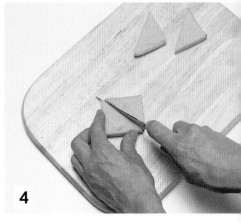

4

Rigatoni with Roasted Beetroot & Rocket

INGREDIENTS

Serves 4

350 g/12 oz raw baby
   beetroot, unpeeled
1 garlic clove, peeled and crushed
½ tsp finely grated orange rind
1 tbsp orange juice
1 tsp lemon juice
2 tbsp walnut oil
salt and freshly ground black pepper
350 g/12 oz dried fettucini
75 g/3 oz rocket leaves
125 g/4 oz Dolcelatte cheese, cut into
   small cubes

1 Preheat oven to 150°C/300°F/Gas Mark 2, 10 minutes before cooking. Wrap the beetroot individually in tinfoil and bake for 1–1½ hours, or until tender. (Test by opening one of the parcels and scraping the skin away from the stem end – it should come off very easily.)

2 Leave the beetroot until cool enough to handle, then peel and cut each beetroot into 6–8 wedges, depending on the size. Mix the garlic, orange rind and juice, lemon juice, walnut oil and salt and pepper together, then drizzle over the beetroot and toss to coat well.

3 Meanwhile, bring a large saucepan of lightly salted water to the boil. Cook the pasta for 10 minutes, or until 'al dente'.

4 Drain the pasta thoroughly, then add the warm beetroot, rocket leaves and Dolcelatte cheese. Quickly and gently toss together, then divide between serving bowls and serve immediately before the rocket wilts.

HELPFUL HINT

Many large supermarkets sell raw beetroot, but baby beetroot may be more readily available from specialist or ethnic greengrocers. Look for beetroot with the leaves attached. The bulbs should be firm without any soft spots and the leaves should not be wilted.

1

2

4

Mixed Salad with Anchovy Dressing & Ciabatta Croûtons

INGREDIENTS

Serves 4

1 small head endive
1 small head chicory
1 fennel bulb
400 g can artichokes, drained and rinsed
½ cucumber
125 g/4 oz cherry tomatoes
75 g/3 oz black olives

For the anchovy dressing:

50 g can anchovy fillets
1 tsp Dijon mustard
1 small garlic clove, peeled and crushed
4 tbsp olive oil
1 tbsp lemon juice
freshly ground black pepper

For the ciabatta croûtons:

2 thick slices ciabatta bread
2 tbsp olive oil

1 Divide the endive and chicory into leaves and reserve some of the larger ones. Arrange the smaller leaves in a wide salad bowl.

2 Cut the fennel bulb in half from the stalk to the root end, then cut across in fine slices. Quarter the artichokes, then quarter and slice the cucumber and halve the tomatoes. Add to the salad bowl with the olives.

3 To make the dressing, drain the anchovies and put in a blender with the mustard, garlic, olive oil, lemon juice, 2 tablespoons of hot water and black pepper. Whiz together until smooth and thickened.

4 To make the croûtons, cut the bread into 1 cm/½ inch cubes. Heat the oil in a frying pan, add the bread cubes and fry for 3 minutes, turning frequently until golden. Remove and drain on absorbent kitchen paper.

5 Drizzle half the anchovy dressing over the prepared salad and toss to coat. Arrange the reserved endive and chicory leaves around the edge, then drizzle over the remaining dressing. Scatter over the croûtons and serve immediately.

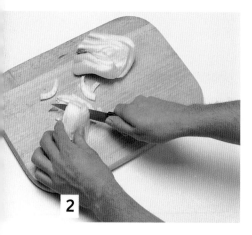
2

3

4

Rice-filled Peppers

INGREDIENTS

Serves 4

8 ripe tomatoes
2 tbsp olive oil
1 onion, peeled and chopped
1 garlic clove, peeled and crushed
½ tsp dark muscovado sugar
125 g/4 oz cooked long-grain rice
50 g/2 oz pine nuts, toasted
1 tbsp freshly chopped oregano
salt and freshly ground black pepper
2 large red peppers
2 large yellow peppers

To serve:

mixed salad
crusty bread

1 Preheat oven to 200°C/400°F/Gas Mark 6. Put the tomatoes in a small bowl and pour over boiling water to cover. Leave for 1 minute, then drain. Plunge the tomatoes into cold water to cool, then peel off the skins. Quarter, remove the seeds and chop.

2 Heat the olive oil in a frying pan, and cook the onion gently for 10 minutes, until softened. Add the garlic, chopped tomatoes and sugar.

3 Gently cook the tomato mixture for 10 minutes until thickened. Remove from the heat and stir the rice, pine nuts and oregano into the sauce. Season to taste with salt and pepper.

4 Halve the peppers lengthways, cutting through and leaving the stem on. Remove the seeds and cores, then put the peppers in a lightly oiled roasting tin, cut-side down and cook in the preheated oven for about 10 minutes.

5 Turn the peppers so they are cut side up. Spoon in the filling, then cover with tinfoil. Return to the oven for 15 minutes, or until the peppers are very tender, removing the tinfoil for the last 5 minutes to allow the tops to brown a little.

6 Serve 1 red pepper half and 1 yellow pepper half per person with a mixed salad and plenty of warmed, crusty bread.

HELPFUL HINT

It may be necessary to take a very thin slice from the bottom of the peppers to enable them to stand on the baking sheet. Be careful not to cut right through.

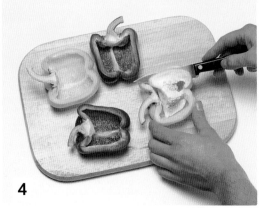

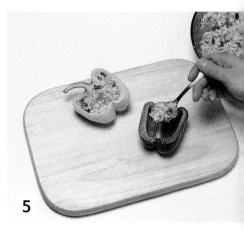

Pasta with Spicy Red Pepper Sauce

INGREDIENTS

Serves 4

2 red peppers
2 tbsp olive oil
1 onion, peeled and chopped
2 garlic cloves, peeled and crushed
4 anchovy fillets
1 red chilli, seeded and
   finely chopped
200 g/7 oz can chopped tomatoes
finely grated rind and juice
   of ½ lemon
salt and freshly ground black pepper
2–3 tbsp vegetable stock (optional)
400 g/14 oz dried pasta, such as
   tagliatelle, linguine or shells

To garnish:
shaved Parmesan cheese
fresh basil leaves

TASTY TIP

If you prefer a chunkier sauce, do not put the peppers through the food processor but finely chop instead. Add to the saucepan with the onion mixture and carry on from step 4.

1 Preheat grill. Set the whole peppers on the grill rack about 10 cm/ 4 inches away from the heat, then grill, turning frequently, for 10 minutes, until the skins are blackened and blistered.

2 Put the peppers in a plastic bag, and leave until cool enough to handle. Peel off the skin, then halve the peppers and scrape away the seeds. Chop the pepper flesh roughly and put in a food processor or blender.

3 Heat the olive oil in a large saucepan and gently fry the onion for 5 minutes. Stir in the garlic, anchovy fillets and chilli and cook for a further 5 minutes, stirring. Add to the food processor and blend until fairly smooth.

4 Return the mixture to the saucepan with the tomatoes and stir in the lemon rind and juice. Season to taste with salt and pepper. Add 2–3 tablespoons of vegetable stock if the sauce is a little thick. Bring to the boil and bubble for 1–2 minutes.

5 Meanwhile, bring a large saucepan of lightly salted water to the boil and cook the pasta for 10 minutes, or until 'al dente'. Drain thoroughly. Add the sauce and toss well to coat.

6 Tip into a warmed serving dish or on to individual plates. Scatter with shavings of Parmesan cheese and a few basil leaves before serving.

1

3

5

Rigatoni with Oven-dried Cherry Tomatoes & Mascarpone

INGREDIENTS

Serves 4

350 g/12 oz red cherry tomatoes
1 tsp caster sugar
salt and freshly ground black pepper
2 tbsp olive oil
400 g/14 oz dried rigatoni
125 g/4 oz petits pois
2 tbsp mascarpone cheese
1 tbsp freshly chopped mint
1 tbsp freshly chopped parsley
sprigs of fresh mint, to garnish

1 Preheat oven to 140°C/275°F/Gas Mark 1. Halve the cherry tomatoes and place close together on a non-stick baking tray, cut-side up. Sprinkle lightly with the sugar, then with a little salt and pepper. Bake in the preheated oven for 1¼ hours, or until dry, but not beginning to colour. Leave to cool on the baking tray. Put in a bowl, drizzle over the olive oil and toss to coat.

2 Bring a large saucepan of lightly salted water to the boil and cook the pasta for about 10 minutes or until 'al dente'. Add the petits pois, 2–3 minutes before the end of the cooking time. Drain thoroughly and return the pasta and the petits pois to the saucepan.

3 Add the mascarpone to the saucepan. When melted, add the tomatoes, mint, parsley and a little black pepper. Toss gently together, then transfer to a warmed serving dish or individual plates and garnish with sprigs of fresh mint. Serve immediately.

TASTY TIP

Double the quantity of tomatoes. When cooked, pack tightly into a sterilised jar layered up with fresh herbs and garlic. Cover with olive oil and leave in the refrigerator for a few days. Use as above or serve as an antipasto with bread, cold meats and olives. Do not keep for longer than 2 weeks.

1

1

2

Red Pepper & Basil Tart

INGREDIENTS

Serves 4

For the olive pastry:

225 g/8 oz plain flour
pinch of salt
50 g/2 oz pitted black olives,
   finely chopped
1 medium egg, lightly beaten, plus
   1 egg yolk
3 tbsp olive oil

For the filling:

2 large red peppers, quartered
   and deseeded
175 g/6 oz mascarpone cheese
4 tbsp milk
2 medium eggs
3 tbsp freshly chopped basil
salt and freshly ground black pepper
sprig of fresh basil, to garnish
mixed salad, to serve

HELPFUL HINT

Pre-baking (or baking blind) the pastry shell before filling is an important step in making any kind of quiche or tart with a moist filling. It ensures that the pastry will not become soggy and that it will be cooked through.

1 Preheat oven to 200°C/400°F/Gas Mark 6, 15 minutes before cooking. Sift the flour and salt into a bowl. Make a well in the centre. Stir together the egg, oil and 1 tablespoon of tepid water. Add to the dry ingredients, drop in the olives and mix to a dough. Knead on a lightly floured surface for a few seconds until smooth, then wrap in clingfilm and chill in the refrigerator for 30 minutes.

2 Roll out the pastry and use to line a 23 cm/9 inch loose-bottomed fluted flan tin. Lightly prick the base with a fork. Cover and chill in the refrigerator for 20 minutes.

3 Cook the peppers under a hot grill for 10 minutes, or until the skins are blackened and blistered. Put the peppers in a plastic bag, cool for 10 minutes, then remove the skin and slice.

4 Line the pastry case with tinfoil or greaseproof paper weighed down with baking beans and bake in the preheated oven for 10 minutes. Remove the tinfoil and beans and bake for a further 5 minutes. Reduce the oven temperature to 180°C/350°F/Gas Mark 4.

5 Beat the mascarpone cheese until smooth. Gradually add the milk and eggs. Stir in the peppers, basil and season to taste with salt and pepper. Spoon into the flan case and bake for 25–30 minutes, or until lightly set. Garnish with a sprig of fresh basil and serve immediately with a mixed salad.

1

3

5

Spinach Dumplings with Rich Tomato Sauce

INGREDIENTS

Serves 4

For the sauce:
2 tbsp olive oil
1 onion, peeled and chopped
1 garlic clove, peeled and crushed
1 red chilli, deseeded and chopped
150 ml/¼ pint dry white wine
400 g can chopped tomatoes
pared strip of lemon rind

For the dumplings:
450 g/1 lb fresh spinach
50 g/2 oz ricotta cheese
25 g/1 oz fresh white breadcrumbs
25 g/1 oz Parmesan cheese, grated
1 medium egg yolk
¼ tsp freshly grated nutmeg
salt and freshly ground black pepper
5 tbsp plain flour
2 tbsp olive oil, for frying
fresh basil leaves, to garnish
freshly cooked tagliatelle, to serve

1 To make the tomato sauce, heat the olive oil in a large saucepan and fry the onion gently for 5 minutes. Add the garlic and chilli and cook for a further 5 minutes, until softened.

2 Stir in the wine, chopped tomatoes and lemon rind. Bring to the boil, cover and simmer for 20 minutes, then uncover and simmer for 15 minutes, or until the sauce has thickened. Remove the lemon rind and season to taste with salt and pepper.

3 To make the spinach dumplings, wash the spinach thoroughly and remove any tough stalks. Cover and cook in a large saucepan over a low heat with just the water clinging to the leaves. Drain, then squeeze out all the excess water. Finely chop and put in a large bowl.

4 Add the ricotta, breadcrumbs, Parmesan cheese and egg yolk to the spinach. Season with nutmeg and salt and pepper. Mix together and shape into 20 walnut-sized balls.

5 Toss the spinach balls in the flour. Heat the olive oil in a large non-stick frying pan and fry the balls gently for 5–6 minutes, carefully turning occasionally. Garnish with fresh basil leaves and serve immediately with the tomato sauce and tagliatelle.

Venetian-style Vegetables & Beans

INGREDIENTS

Serves 4

250 g/9 oz dried pinto beans
3 sprigs of fresh parsley
1 sprig of fresh rosemary
2 tbsp olive oil
200 g can chopped tomatoes
2 shallots, peeled

For the vegetable mixture:

1 large red onion, peeled
1 large white onion, peeled
1 medium carrot, peeled
2 sticks celery, trimmed
3 tbsp olive oil
3 bay leaves
1 tsp caster sugar
3 tbsp red wine vinegar
salt and freshly ground black pepper

HELPFUL HINT

If time is short, put the beans into a large saucepan and cover with cold water. Bring to the boil and boil rapidly for 10 minutes. Turn off the heat and leave to stand for 2 hours. Drain well and cover with fresh water. Cook as above.

1 Put the beans in a bowl, cover with plenty of cold water and leave to soak for at least 8 hours, or overnight.

2 Drain and rinse the beans. Put in a large saucepan with 1.1 litres/ 2 pints cold water. Tie the parsley and rosemary in muslin and add to the beans with the olive oil. Boil rapidly for 10 minutes, then lower the heat and simmer for 20 minutes with the saucepan half-covered. Stir in the tomatoes and shallots and simmer for a further 10–15 minutes, or until the beans are cooked.

3 Meanwhile, slice the red and white onion into rings and then finely dice the carrot and celery. Heat the olive oil in a saucepan and cook the onions over a very low heat for about 10 minutes. Add the carrot, celery and bay leaves to the saucepan and cook for a further 10 minutes, stirring frequently, until the vegetables are tender. Sprinkle with sugar, stir and cook for 1 minute.

4 Stir in the vinegar. Cook for 1 minute, then remove the saucepan from the heat. Drain the beans through a fine sieve, discarding all the herbs, then add the beans to the onion mixture and season well with salt and pepper. Mix gently, then tip the beans into a large serving bowl. Leave to cool, then serve at room temperature.

2

2

3

Roast Butternut Squash Risotto

INGREDIENTS

Serves 4

1 medium butternut squash
2 tbsp olive oil
1 garlic bulb, cloves separated,
  but unpeeled
15 g/½ oz unsalted butter
275 g/10 oz Arborio rice
large pinch of saffron strands
150 ml/¼ pint dry white wine
1 litre/1¾ pints vegetable stock
1 tbsp freshly chopped parsley
1 tbsp freshly chopped oregano
50 g/2 oz Parmesan cheese,
  finely grated
salt and freshly ground black pepper
sprigs of fresh oregano, to garnish
extra Parmesan cheese, to serve

1 Preheat oven to 190°C/375°F/Gas Mark 5. Cut the butternut squash in half, thickly peel, then scoop out the seeds and discard. Cut the flesh into 2 cm/¾ inch cubes.

2 Pour the oil into a large roasting tin and heat in the preheated oven for 5 minutes. Add the butternut squash and garlic cloves. Turn in the oil to coat, then roast in the oven for about 25–30 minutes, or until golden brown and very tender, turning the vegetables halfway through cooking time.

3 Melt the butter in a large saucepan. Add the rice and stir over a high heat for a few seconds. Add the saffron and the wine and bubble fiercely until almost totally reduced, stirring frequently. At the same time heat the stock in a separate saucepan and keep at a steady simmer.

4 Reduce the heat under the rice to low. Add a ladleful of stock to the saucepan and simmer, stirring, until absorbed. Continue adding the stock in this way until the rice is tender. This will take about 20 minutes and it may not be necessary to add all the stock.

5 Turn off the heat, stir in the herbs, Parmesan cheese and seasoning. Cover and leave to stand for 2–3 minutes. Quickly remove the skins from the roasted garlic. Add to the risotto with the butternut squash and mix gently. Garnish with sprigs of oregano and serve immediately with Parmesan cheese.

HELPFUL HINT

It is important to keep the stock simmering alongside the risotto because this ensures that the cooking process is not interrupted.

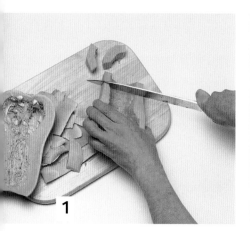
1

2

4

Hot Grilled Chicory & Pears

INGREDIENTS

Serves 4

50 g/2 oz unblanched almonds,
   roughly chopped
4 small heads of chicory
2 tbsp olive oil
1 tbsp walnut oil
2 firm ripe dessert pears
2 tsp lemon juice
1 tsp freshly chopped oregano.
salt and freshly ground black pepper
freshly chopped oregano, to garnish
warmed ciabatta bread, to serve

1 Preheat grill. Spread the chopped almonds in a single layer on the grill pan. Cook under a hot grill for about 3 minutes, moving the almonds around occasionally, until lightly browned. Reserve.

2 Halve the chicory lengthways and cut out the cores. Mix together the olive and walnut oils. Brush about 2 tablespoons all over the chicory.

3 Put the chicory in a grill pan, cut-side up and cook under a hot grill for 2–3 minutes, or until beginning to char. Turn and cook for a further 1–2 minutes, then turn again.

4 Peel, core and thickly slice the pears. Brush with 1 tablespoon of the oils, then place the pears on top of the chicory. Grill for a further 3–4 minutes, or until both the chicory and pears are soft.

5 Transfer the chicory and pears to 4 warmed serving plates. Whisk together the remaining oil, lemon juice and oregano and season to taste with salt and pepper.

6 Drizzle the dressing over the chicory and pears and scatter with the toasted almonds. Garnish with fresh oregano and serve with ciabatta bread.

HELPFUL HINT

If preparing the pears ahead of time for this recipe, dip or brush them with some lemon juice to ensure that they do not discolour before cooking.

1

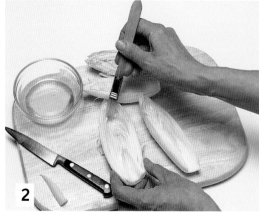

2

4

Aubergine Cannelloni with Watercress Sauce

INGREDIENTS

Serves 4

4 large aubergines, about
   250 g/9 oz each
5–6 tbsp olive oil
350 g/12 oz ricotta cheese
75 g/3 oz Parmesan cheese, grated
3 tbsp freshly chopped basil
salt and freshly ground black pepper

For the watercress sauce:

75 g/3 oz watercress, trimmed
200 ml/⅓ pint vegetable stock
1 shallot, peeled and sliced
pared strip of lemon rind
1 large sprig of thyme
3 tbsp crème fraîche
1 tsp lemon juice

To garnish:

sprigs of watercress
lemon zest

1 Preheat oven to 190°C/375°F/Gas Mark 5, 10 minutes before cooking. Cut the aubergines lengthways into thin slices, discarding the side pieces. Heat 2 tablespoons of oil in a frying pan and cook the aubergine slices in a single layer in several batches, turning once, until golden on both sides.

2 Mix the cheeses, basil and seasoning together. Lay the aubergine slices on a clean surface and spread the cheese mixture evenly between them.

3 Roll up the slices from one of the short ends to enclose the filling. Place, seam-side down in a single layer in an ovenproof dish. Bake in the preheated oven for 15 minutes, or until golden.

4 To make the watercress sauce, blanch the watercress leaves in boiling water for about 30 seconds. Drain well, then rinse in a sieve under cold running water and squeeze dry. Put the stock, shallot, lemon rind and thyme in a small saucepan. Boil rapidly until reduced by half, then remove from the heat and strain.

5 Put the watercress and strained stock in a food processor and blend until fairly smooth. Return to the saucepan, stir in the crème fraîche, lemon juice and season to taste with salt and pepper. Heat gently until the sauce is piping hot.

6 Serve a little of the sauce drizzled over the aubergines and the rest separately in a jug. Garnish the cannelloni with sprigs of watercress and lemon zest. Serve immediately.

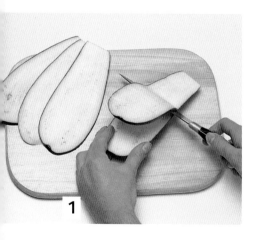
1

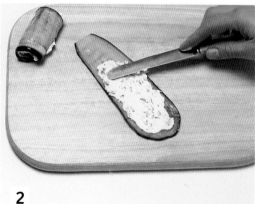
2

5

Panzanella

INGREDIENTS

Serves 4

250 g/9 oz day-old Italian-style bread
1 tbsp red wine vinegar
4 tbsp olive oil
1 tsp lemon juice
1 small garlic clove, peeled and
   finely chopped
1 red onion, peeled and finely sliced
1 cucumber, peeled if preferred
225 g/8 oz ripe tomatoes, deseeded
150 g/5 oz pitted black olives
about 20 basil leaves, coarsely torn
   or left whole if small
sea salt and freshly ground
   black pepper

1 Cut the bread into thick slices, leaving the crusts on. Add 1 teaspoon of red wine vinegar to a jug of iced water, put the slices of bread in a bowl and pour over the water. Make sure the bread is covered completely. Leave to soak for 3–4 minutes until just soft.

2 Remove the soaked bread from the water and squeeze it gently, first with your hands and then in a clean tea towel to remove any excess water. Put the bread on a plate, cover with clingfilm and chill in the refrigerator for about 1 hour.

3 Meanwhile, whisk together the olive oil, the remaining red wine vinegar and lemon juice in a large serving bowl. Add the garlic and onion and stir to coat well.

4 Halve the cucumber and remove the seeds. Chop both the cucumber and tomatoes into 1 cm/½ inch dice. Add to the garlic and onions with the olives. Tear the bread into bite-sized chunks and add to the bowl with the fresh basil leaves. Toss together to mix and serve immediately, with a grinding of sea salt and black pepper.

TASTY TIP

Choose an open-textured Italian-style bread such as ciabatta for this classic Tuscan salad. Look in your local delicatessen for different flavoured marinated olives. Try chilli and garlic, or basil, garlic and orange.

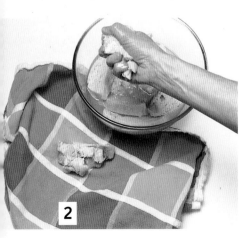

2

3

4

Vegetable Frittata

INGREDIENTS

Serves 2

6 medium eggs

2 tbsp freshly chopped parsley

1 tbsp freshly chopped tarragon

25 g/1 oz pecorino or Parmesan
cheese, finely grated

freshly ground black pepper

175 g/6 oz tiny new potatoes

2 small carrots, peeled and sliced

125 g/4 oz broccoli, cut into
small florets

1 courgette, about 125 g/4 oz, sliced

2 tbsp olive oil

4 spring onions, trimmed and
thinly sliced

To serve:

mixed green salad

crusty Italian bread

FOOD FACT

A frittata is a heavy omelette,
usually with a vegetable, meat or
cheese filling that is cooked slowly
and often finished in the oven or
under the grill. It is closer to a
Spanish tortilla than to a classic
French omelette.

1 Preheat grill just before cooking. Lightly beat the eggs with the parsley, tarragon and half the cheese. Season to taste with black pepper and reserve. (Salt is not needed as the pecorino is very salty.)

2 Bring a large saucepan of lightly salted water to the boil. Add the new potatoes and cook for 8 minutes. Add the carrots and cook for 4 minutes, then add the broccoli florets and the courgettes and cook for a further 3–4 minutes, or until all the vegetables are barely tender. Drain well.

3 Heat the oil in a 20.5 cm/8 inch heavy-based frying pan. Add the spring onions and cook for 3–4 minutes, or until softened. Add all the vegetables and cook for a few seconds, then pour in the beaten egg mixture.

4 Stir gently for about a minute, then cook for a further 1–2 minutes, or until the bottom of the frittata is set and golden brown.

5 Place the pan under a hot grill for 1 minute, or until almost set and just beginning to brown. Sprinkle with the remaining cheese and grill for a further 1 minute, or until it is lightly browned.

6 Loosen the edges and slide out of the pan. Cut into wedges and serve hot or warm with a mixed green salad and crusty Italian bread.

2

3

5

Panzerotti

INGREDIENTS

Serves 16

450 g/1 lb strong white flour
pinch of salt
1 tsp easy-blend dried yeast
2 tbsp olive oil
300 ml/½ pint warm water
fresh rocket leaves, to serve

For the filling:

1 tbsp olive oil
1 small red onion, peeled and
   finely chopped
2 garlic cloves, peeled and crushed
½ yellow pepper, deseeded
   and chopped
1 small courgette, about 75 g/
   3 oz, trimmed and chopped
50 g/2 oz black olives, pitted
   and quartered
125 g/4 oz mozzarella cheese,
   cut into tiny cubes
salt and freshly ground black pepper
5–6 tbsp tomato purée
1 tsp dried mixed herbs
oil for deep-frying

1 Sift the flour and salt into a bowl. Stir in the yeast. Make a well in the centre. Add the oil and the warm water and mix to a soft dough. Knead on a lightly floured surface until smooth and elastic. Put in an oiled bowl, cover and leave in a warm place to rise while making the filling.

2 To make the filling, heat the oil in a frying pan and cook the onion for 5 minutes. Add the garlic, yellow pepper and courgette. Cook for about 5 minutes, or until the vegetables are tender. Tip into a bowl and leave to cool slightly. Stir in the olives, mozzarella cheese and season to taste with salt and pepper.

3 Briefly reknead the dough. Divide into 16 equal pieces. Roll out each to a circle about 10 cm/4 inches. Mix together the tomato purée and dried herbs, then spread about 1 teaspoon on each circle, leaving a 2 cm/¾ inch border around the edge.

4 Divide the filling equally between the circles, it will seem a small amount, but if you overfill, they will leak during cooking. Brush the edges with water, then fold in half to enclose the filling. Press to seal, then crimp the edges.

5 Heat the oil in a deep-fat fryer to 180°C/350°F. Deep-fry the panzerotti in batches for 3 minutes, or until golden. Drain on absorbent kitchen paper and keep warm in a low oven until ready to serve with fresh rocket.

1

2

4

Pasta Primavera

INGREDIENTS

Serves 4

150 g/5 oz French beans
150 g/5 oz sugar snap peas
40 g/1½ oz butter
1 tsp olive oil
225 g/8 oz baby carrots, scrubbed
2 courgettes, trimmed and
  thinly sliced
175 g/6 oz baby leeks, trimmed and
  cut into 2.5 cm/1 inch lengths
200 ml/7 fl oz double cream
1 tsp finely grated lemon rind
350 g/12 oz dried tagliatelle
25 g/1 oz Parmesan cheese, grated
1 tbsp freshly snipped chives
1 tbsp freshly chopped dill
salt and freshly ground black pepper
sprigs of fresh dill, to garnish

1 Trim and halve the French beans. Bring a large saucepan of lightly salted water to the boil and cook the beans for 4–5 minutes, adding the sugar snap peas after 2 minutes, so that both are tender at the same time. Drain the beans and sugar snap peas and briefly rinse under cold running water.

2 Heat the butter and oil in a large non-stick frying pan. Add the baby carrots and cook for 2 minutes, then stir in the courgettes and leeks and cook for 10 minutes, stirring, until the vegetables are almost tender.

3 Stir the cream and lemon rind into the vegetables and bubble over a gentle heat until the sauce is slightly reduced and the vegetables are cooked.

4 Meanwhile, bring a large saucepan of lightly salted water to the boil and cook the tagliatelle for 10 minutes, or until 'al dente'.

5 Add the beans, sugar snaps, Parmesan cheese and herbs to the sauce. Stir for 30 seconds, or until the cheese has melted and the vegetables are hot.

6 Drain the tagliatelle, add the vegetables and sauce, then toss gently to mix and season to taste with salt and pepper. Spoon into a warmed serving bowl and garnish with a few sprigs of dill and serve immediately.

FOOD FACT

Primavera means 'spring' and this dish is classically made with spring vegetables. At other times, use available baby vegetables.

2

5

6

Vanilla & Lemon Panna Cotta with Raspberry Sauce

INGREDIENTS

Serves 6

900 ml/1½ pints double cream
1 vanilla pod, split
100 g/3½ oz caster sugar
zest of 1 lemon
3 sheets gelatine
5 tbsp milk
450 g/1 lb raspberries
3–4 tbsp icing sugar, to taste
1 tbsp lemon juice
extra lemon zest, to decorate

TASTY TIP

Sheet gelatine is readily available from large supermarkets. It is much easier to measure and use than powdered gelatine and also gives a glossier finish to clear jellies.

1   Put the cream, vanilla pod and sugar into a saucepan. Bring to the boil, then simmer for 10 minutes until slightly reduced, stirring to prevent scalding. Remove from the heat, stir in the lemon zest and remove the vanilla pod.

2   Soak the gelatine in the milk for 5 minutes, or until softened. Squeeze out any excess milk and add to the hot cream. Stir well until dissolved.

3   Pour the cream mixture into 6 ramekins or mini pudding moulds and leave in the refrigerator for 4 hours, or until set.

4   Meanwhile, put 175 g/6 oz of the raspberries in a food processor with the icing sugar and lemon juice. Blend to a purée then pass the mixture through a sieve. Fold in the remaining raspberries with a metal spoon or rubber spatula and chill in the refrigerator until ready to serve.

5   To serve, dip each of the moulds into hot water for a few seconds, then turn out on to 6 individual serving plates. Spoon some of the raspberry sauce over and around the panna cotta, decorate with extra lemon zest and serve.

1

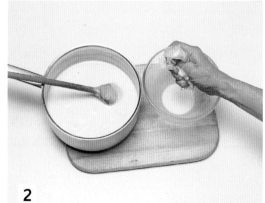

2

4

Ricotta Cheesecake with Strawberry Coulis

INGREDIENTS

Serves 6

125 g/4 oz digestive biscuits
100 g/3½ oz candied peel, chopped
65 g/2½ oz butter, melted
150 ml/¼ pint crème fraîche
575 g/4 oz ricotta cheese
100 g/3½ oz caster sugar
1 vanilla pod, seeds only
2 large eggs
225 g/8 oz strawberries
25–50 g/1–2 oz caster sugar, to taste
zest and juice of 1 orange

1 Preheat oven to 170°C/325°F/Gas Mark 3. Line a 20.5 cm/8 inch springform tin with baking parchment. Place the biscuits into a food processor together with the peel. Blend until the biscuits are crushed and the peel is chopped. Add 50 g/2 oz of the melted butter and process until mixed. Tip into the tin and spread evenly over the bottom. Press firmly into place and reserve.

2 Blend together the crème fraîche, ricotta cheese, sugar, vanilla seeds and eggs in a food processor. With the motor running, add the remaining melted butter and blend for a few seconds. Pour the mixture on to the base. Transfer to the preheated oven and cook for about 1 hour, until set and risen round the edges, but slightly wobbly in the centre. Switch off the oven and allow to cool there. Chill in the refrigerator for at least 8 hours, or preferably overnight.

3 Wash and drain the strawberries. Hull the fruit and remove any soft spots. Put into the food processor along with 25 g/1 oz of the sugar and orange juice and zest. Blend until smooth. Add the remaining sugar to taste. Pass through a sieve to remove seeds and chill in the refrigerator until needed.

4 Cut the cheesecake into wedges, spoon over some of the strawberry coulis and serve.

TASTY TIP

This cheesecake has a soft, creamy texture compared to some baked cheesecakes. This is because of the addition of crème fraîche. If ricotta is unavailable, substitute with full-fat soft cheese.

1

2

3

Cantuccini

INGREDIENTS

Makes 24 biscuits

250 g/9 oz plain flour
250 g/9 oz caster sugar
½ tsp baking powder
½ tsp vanilla essence
2 medium eggs
1 medium egg yolk
100 g/3½ oz mixed almonds
   and hazelnuts, toasted and
   roughly chopped
1 tsp whole aniseed
1 medium egg yolk mixed with
   1 tbsp water, to glaze
Vin Santo or coffee, to serve

1 Preheat oven to 180°C/350°F/Gas Mark 4. Line a large baking sheet with non-stick baking parchment. Place the flour, caster sugar, baking powder, vanilla essence, the whole eggs and one of the egg yolks into a food processor and blend until the mixture forms a ball, scraping down the sides once or twice. Turn the mixture out on to a lightly floured surface and knead in the chopped nuts and aniseed.

2 Divide the paste into 3 pieces and roll into logs about 4 cm/ 1½ inches wide. Place the logs on to the baking sheet at least 5 cm/2 inches apart. Brush lightly with the other egg yolk beaten with 1 tablespoon of water and bake in the preheated oven for 30–35 minutes.

3 Remove from the oven and reduce the oven temperature to 150°C/300°F/Gas Mark 2. Cut the logs diagonally into 2.5 cm/ 1 inch slices and lay cut-side down on the baking sheet. Return to the oven for a further 30–40 minutes, or until dry and firm. Cool on a wire rack and store in an airtight container. Serve with Vin Santo or coffee.

FOOD FACT

Cantuccini are simply small biscuits, traditionally served with a sweet dessert wine called Vin Santo. Cantucci are large biscuits that are made in the same way.

1

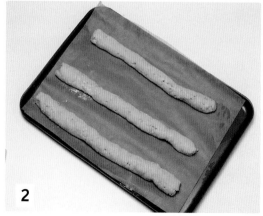

2

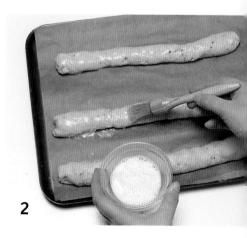

2

Almond & Pistachio Biscotti

INGREDIENTS

Makes 12 biscuits

125 g/4 oz ground almonds
50 g/2 oz shelled pistachios
50 g/2 oz blanched almonds
2 medium eggs
1 medium egg yolk
125 g/4 oz icing sugar
225 g/8 oz plain flour
1 tsp baking powder
pinch of salt
zest of ½ lemon

TASTY TIP

These biscuits are also delicious made with a single kind of nut – try hazelnuts or just almonds. When toasting nuts spread them out on a baking sheet then place in a preheated oven at 200°C/400°F/Gas Mark 6. Leave for 5–10 minutes, stirring occasionally. If using a lower temperature, leave for a few more minutes.

1 Preheat oven to 180°C/350°F/Gas Mark 4. Line a large baking sheet with non-stick baking parchment. Toast the ground almonds and whole nuts lightly and reserve until cool.

2 Beat together the eggs, egg yolk and icing sugar until thick, then beat in the flour, baking powder and salt. Add the lemon zest, ground almonds and whole nuts and mix to form a slightly sticky dough.

3 Turn the dough on to a lightly floured surface and, using lightly floured hands, form into a log measuring approximately 30 cm/ 12 inches long. Place down the centre of the prepared baking sheet and transfer to the preheated oven. Bake for 20 minutes.

4 Remove from the oven and increase the oven temperature to 200°C/400°F/Gas Mark 6. Cut the log diagonally into 2.5 cm/1 inch slices. Return to the baking sheet, cut-side down and bake for a further 10–15 minutes until golden, turning once after 10 minutes. Leave to cool on a wire rack and store in an airtight container.

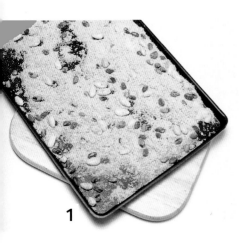

2

1

4

Hazelnut, Chocolate & Chestnut Meringue Torte

INGREDIENTS

Serves 8–10

For the chocolate meringue:

1 medium egg white

50 g/2 oz caster sugar

2 tbsp cocoa powder

For the hazelnut meringue:

75 g/3 oz hazelnuts, toasted

2 medium egg whites

125 g/4 oz caster sugar

For the filling:

300 ml/½ pint double cream

250 g can sweetened chestnut purée

50 g/2 oz plain dark chocolate, melted

25 g/1 oz plain dark chocolate, grated

1 Preheat oven to 130°C/250°F/Gas Mark ½. Line 3 baking sheets with non-stick baking parchment and draw a 20.5 cm/8 inch circle on each. Beat 1 egg white until stiff peaks form. Add 25 g/1 oz of the sugar and beat until shiny. Mix the cocoa with the remaining 25 g/1 oz of sugar and add 1 tablespoon at a time, beating well after each addition, until all the sugar is added and the mixture is stiff and glossy. Spread on to 1 of the baking sheets within the circle drawn on the underside.

2 Put the hazelnuts in a food processor and blend until chopped. In a clean bowl, beat the 2 egg whites until stiff. Add 50 g/2 oz of the sugar and beat. Add the remaining sugar about 1 tablespoon at a time, beating after each addition until all the sugar is added and the mixture is stiff and glossy.

3 Reserve 2 tablespoons of the nuts, then fold in the remainder and divide between the 2 remaining baking sheets. Sprinkle one of the hazelnut meringues with the reserved hazelnuts and transfer all the baking sheets to the oven. Bake in the preheated oven for 1½ hours. Turn the oven off and leave in the oven until cold.

4 Whip the cream until thick. Beat the chestnut purée in another bowl until soft. Add a spoonful of the cream and fold together before adding the remaining cream and melted chocolate and fold together.

5 Place the plain hazelnut meringue on a serving plate. Top with half the cream and chestnut mixture. Add the chocolate meringue and top with the remaining cream. Add the final meringue. Sprinkle over the grated chocolate and serve.

1

1

4

Bomba Siciliana

INGREDIENTS

Serves 6–8

100 g/3½ oz plain chocolate,
  broken into pieces
200 g/7 oz fresh chilled custard
150 ml/¼ pint whipping cream
25 g/1 oz candied peel,
  finely chopped
25 g/1 oz glacé cherries, chopped
25 g/1 oz sultanas
3 tbsp rum
225 g/8 oz good-quality vanilla
  ice cream
200 ml/¼ pint double cream
3 tbsp caster sugar

1 Melt the plain chocolate in bowl set over a saucepan of simmering water until smooth, then cool. Whisk together the custard with the whipping cream and slightly cooled chocolate. Spoon the mixture into a shallow, lidded freezer box and freeze. Every 2 hours, remove from the freezer and using an electric whisk or balloon whisk, whisk thoroughly. Repeat 3 times, then leave until frozen solid. Soak the candied peel, cherries and sultanas in the rum and leave until needed.

2 Chill a bombe or 1 litre/¾ pint pudding mould in the freezer for about 30 minutes. Remove the chocolate ice cream from the freezer to soften, then spoon the ice cream into the mould and press down well, smoothing around the edges and leaving a hollow in the centre. Return the ice cream to the freezer for about 1 hour, or until frozen hard.

3 Remove the vanilla ice cream from the freezer to soften. Spoon the softened vanilla ice cream into the hollow, making sure to leave another hollow for the cream. Return to the freezer again and freeze until hard.

4 Whip the cream and sugar until it is just holding its shape then fold in the soaked fruit. Remove the mould from the freezer and spoon in the cream mixture. Return to the freezer for at least another hour.

5 When ready to serve, remove the mould from the freezer and dip into hot water for a few seconds, then turn on to a large serving plate. Dip a knife into hot water and cut into wedges to serve.

TASTY TIP

For the best flavour, buy whole candied peel. Cut it into strips using kitchen scissors, then chop crosswise into small pieces.

1

1

2

Summer Fruit Semifreddo

INGREDIENTS

Serves 6–8

225 g/8 oz raspberries
125 g/4 oz blueberries
125 g/4 oz redcurrants
50 g/2 oz icing sugar
juice of 1 lemon
1 vanilla pod, split
50 g/2 oz sugar
4 large eggs, separated
600 ml/1 pint double cream
pinch of salt
fresh redcurrants, to decorate

1 Wash and hull or remove stalks from the fruits, as necessary, then put them into a food processor or blender with the icing sugar and lemon juice. Blend to a purée, pour into a jug and chill in the refrigerator, until needed.

2 Remove the seeds from the vanilla pod by opening the pod and scraping with the back of a knife. Add the seeds to the sugar and whisk with the egg yolks until pale and thick.

3 In another bowl, whip the cream until soft peaks form. Do not overwhip. In a third bowl, whip the egg whites with the salt until stiff peaks form.

4 Using a large metal spoon – to avoid knocking any air from the mixture – fold together the fruit purée, egg yolk mixture, the cream and egg whites. Transfer the mixture to a round, shallow, lidded freezer box and put into the freezer until almost frozen. If the mixture freezes solid, thaw in the refrigerator until semi-frozen. Turn out the semi-frozen mixture, cut into wedges and serve decorated with a few fresh redcurrants. If the mixture thaws completely, eat immediately and do not refreeze.

TASTY TIP

Use the egg and cream mixture as the basis for a host of other flavours, such as praline, chocolate or autumn berries.

1

2

4

Cassatta

INGREDIENTS

Serves 6–8

300 g/11 oz plain chocolate,
  broken into pieces

200 g/7 oz fresh chilled custard

150 ml/¹/₄ pint whipping cream

275 g/10 oz good-quality pistachio
  ice cream

25 g/1 oz shelled pistachios, toasted

50 g/2 oz candied peel,
  finely chopped

25 g/1 oz glacé cherries,
  finely chopped

275 g/10 oz good-quality strawberry
  ice cream

TASTY TIP

To make your own pistachio ice cream, toast 50 g/2 oz of shelled pistachios and when cold, chop finely. Follow the recipe for chocolate ice cream above, omitting the chocolate and folding in the nuts along with the cream. Add a few drops of green food colour, if liked.

1 Line a 450 g/1 lb loaf tin with clingfilm. Place in the freezer. Melt 100 g/3¹/₂ oz of the chocolate into a heatproof bowl set over a saucepan of simmering water, stir until smooth, then cool. Place the custard into a bowl. Stir in the cream and the chocolate and stir until mixed. Spoon into a shallow, lidded freezer box and transfer to the freezer. Every 2 hours remove from the freezer and using an electric whisk, whisk thoroughly. Repeat 3 times, then leave until frozen solid.

2 Remove the chocolate ice cream from the freezer and allow to soften. Remove the loaf tin from the freezer and press the chocolate ice cream into the bottom of the tin, press down well and allow it to come up the sides of the tin. Return to the freezer and leave until solid.

3 Soften the pistachio ice cream, then beat in the pistachios, candied peel and cherries. Spoon into the tin, pressing down well and smoothing the top. Return to the freezer until hard. Soften the strawberry ice cream and spread on to the pistachio ice cream. Smooth the top. Return to the freezer for at least 1 hour, or until completely solid.

4 Meanwhile, melt the remaining chocolate, stir until smooth and cool slightly. Remove the loaf tin from the freezer. Dip into hot water and turn on to a serving dish. Using a teaspoon, drizzle the chocolate over the ice cream in a haphazard pattern. Return the cassatta to the freezer, until the chocolate has set. Dip a knife in hot water and use to slice the cassatta. Serve immediately.

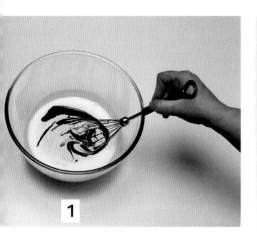

1

3

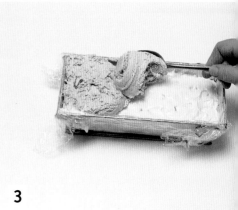

3

Marzipan Cake

INGREDIENTS

Serves 12–14

450 g/1 lb blanched almonds

300 g/11 oz icing sugar (includes sugar for dusting and rolling)

4 medium egg whites

125 g/4 oz Madeira cake

2 tbsp Marsala wine

225 g/8 oz ricotta cheese

50 g/2 oz caster sugar

grated zest of 1 lemon

50 g/2 oz candied peel, finely chopped

25 g/1 oz glacé cherries, finely chopped

425 g can peach halves, drained

200 ml/⅓ pint double cream

1 Grind the blanched almonds in a food processor until fairly fine. Mix with 200 g/7 oz of the icing sugar. Beat the egg whites until stiff then fold into the almond mixture using a metal spoon or rubber spatula to form a stiffish dough. It will still be quite sticky but will firm up as it rests. Leave for 30 minutes.

2 Dust a work surface very generously with some of the remaining icing sugar so that the marzipan does not stick. Roll out two-thirds of the marzipan into a large sheet to a thickness of about 5 mm/ ¼ inch. Use to line a sloping-sided baking dish with a base measuring 25.5 cm x 20.5 cm/10 x 8 inches. Trim the edges and put any trimmings with the remainder of the marzipan.

3 Cut the Madeira cake into thin slices and make a layer of sponge to cover the bottom of the marzipan. Sprinkle with the Marsala wine. Beat the ricotta with the sugar and add the lemon zest, candied peel and cherries. Spread this over the sponge. Slice the peaches and put them on top of the ricotta. Whip the cream and spread it over the peaches. Roll out the remaining marzipan and lay it over the cream to seal the whole cake, pressing down gently to remove any air. Press the edges of the marzipan together. Chill in the refrigerator for 2 hours.

4 Turn the cake out on to a serving plate and dust generously with icing sugar. Slice thickly and serve immediately.

HELPFUL HINT

Homemade marzipan is stickier than commercially prepared versions. Use plenty of icing sugar when rolling it as well as sprinkling the dish liberally with it.

1

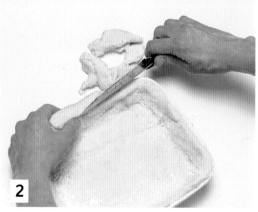

2

3

Chestnut Cake

INGREDIENTS

Serves 8–10

175 g/6 oz butter, softened
175 g/6 oz caster sugar
250 g can sweetened chestnut purée
3 medium eggs, lightly beaten
175 g/6 oz plain flour
1 tsp baking powder
pinch of ground cloves
1 tsp fennel seeds, crushed
75 g/3 oz raisins
50 g/2 oz pine nuts, toasted
125 g/4 oz icing sugar
5 tbsp lemons juice
pared strips of lemon rind,
  to decorate

TASTY TIP

To toast pine nuts spread them on to a large baking sheet and transfer to a preheated oven 200°C/400°F/Gas Mark 6. Bake for about 3–5 minutes, checking often as they burn very easily. Remove the toasted pine nuts from the oven, tip on to a plate and leave to cool, then use as required.

1 Preheat oven to 150°C/300°F/Gas Mark 2. Oil and line a 23 cm/ 9 inch springform tin. Beat together the butter and sugar until light and fluffy. Add the chestnut purée and beat. Gradually add the eggs, beating after each addition. Sift in the flour with the baking powder and cloves. Add the fennel seeds and beat. The mixture should drop easily from a wooden spoon when tapped against the side of the bowl. If not, add a little milk.

2 Beat in the raisins and pine nuts. Spoon the mixture into the prepared tin and smooth the top. Transfer to the centre of the oven and bake in the preheated oven for 55–60 minutes, or until a skewer inserted in the centre of the cake comes out clean. Remove from the oven and leave in the tin.

3 Meanwhile, mix together the icing sugar and lemon juice in a small saucepan until smooth. Heat gently until hot, but not boiling. Using a cocktail stick or skewer, poke holes into the cake all over. Pour the hot syrup evenly over the cake and leave to soak into the cake. Decorate with pared strips of lemon and serve.

1

2

3

Sauternes & Olive Oil Cake

INGREDIENTS

Serves 8–10

125 g/4 oz plain flour, plus extra
  for dusting
4 medium eggs
125 g/4 oz caster sugar
grated zest of ½ lemon
grated zest of ½ orange
2 tbsp Sauternes or other sweet
  dessert wine
3 tbsp very best quality
  extra-virgin olive oil
4 ripe peaches
1–2 tsp soft brown sugar,
  or to taste
1 tbsp lemon juice
icing sugar, to dust

1 Preheat oven to 140°C/275°F/Gas Mark 1. Oil and line a 25.5 cm/ 10 inch springform tin. Sift the flour on to a large sheet of greaseproof paper and reserve. Using a freestanding electric mixer, if possible, whisk the eggs and sugar together, until pale and stiff. Add the lemon and orange zest.

2 Turn the speed to low and pour the flour from the paper in a slow, steady stream on to the eggs and sugar mixture. Immediately add the wine and olive oil and switch the machine off as the olive oil should not be incorporated completely.

3 Using a rubber spatula, fold the mixture very gently 3 or 4 times so that the ingredients are just incorporated. Pour the mixture immediately into the prepared tin and bake in the preheated oven for 20–25 minutes, without opening the door for at least 15 minutes. Test if cooked by pressing the top lightly with a clean finger – if it springs back, remove from the oven, if not, bake for a little longer.

4 Leave the cake to cool in the tin on a wire rack. Remove the cake from the tin when cool enough to handle.

5 Meanwhile, skin the peaches and cut into segments. Toss with the brown sugar and lemon juice and reserve. When the cake is cold, dust generously with icing sugar, cut into wedges and serve with the peaches.

HELPFUL HINT

Be careful in step 3 when folding the mixture together not to overmix or the finished cake will be very heavy.

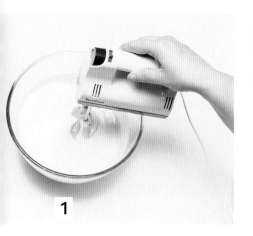

1

2

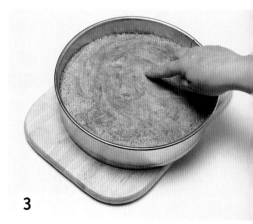

3

Frozen Amaretti Soufflé with Strawberries

INGREDIENTS

Serves 6–8

125 g/4 oz Amaretti biscuits
9 tbsp Amaretto liqueur
grated zest and juice of 1 lemon
1 tbsp powdered gelatine
6 medium eggs, separated
175 g/6 oz soft brown sugar
600 ml/1 pint double cream
450 g/1 lb fresh strawberries,
   halved if large
1 vanilla pod, split and seeds
   scraped out
2 tbsp caster sugar
few finely crushed Amaretti
   biscuits, to decorate

HELPFUL HINT

When making ice cream it is important to set the freezer to rapid freeze at least 2 hours beforehand. Remember to return the freezer to its normal setting when you have finished.

1 Wrap a collar of greaseproof paper around a 900 ml/1½ pint soufflé dish or 6–8 individual ramekin dishes to extend at least 5 cm/2 inch above the rim and secure with string. Break the Amaretti biscuits into a bowl. Sprinkle over 6 tablespoons of the Amaretto liqueur and leave to soak.

2 Put the lemon zest and juice into a small heatproof bowl and sprinkle over the gelatine. Leave for 5 minutes to sponge, then put the bowl over a saucepan of simmering water, ensuring that the base of the bowl does not touch the water. Stir occasionally until the gelatine has dissolved completely.

3 In a clean bowl, whisk the egg yolks and sugar until pale and thick then stir in the gelatine and the soaked biscuits. In another bowl, lightly whip 450 ml/¾ pint of the cream and using a large metal spoon or rubber spatula fold into the mixture. In a third clean bowl, whisk the egg whites until stiff, then fold into the soufflé mixture. Transfer to the prepared dish, or individual ramekin dishes, and level the top. Freeze for at least 8 hours, or preferably overnight.

4 Put the strawberries into a bowl with the vanilla pod and seeds, sugar and remaining Amaretto liqueur. Leave overnight in the refrigerator, then allow to come to room temperature before serving.

5 Place the soufflé in the refrigerator for about 1 hour. Whip the remaining cream and use to decorate the soufflé then sprinkle a few finely crushed Amaretti biscuits on the top and serve with the strawberries.

1

2

3

Baked Stuffed Amaretti Peaches

INGREDIENTS

Serves 4

4 ripe peaches
grated zest and juice of 1 lemon
75 g/3 oz Amaretti biscuits
50 g/2 oz chopped blanched
   almonds, toasted
50 g/2 oz pine nuts, toasted
40 g/1½ oz light muscovado sugar
50 g/2 oz butter
1 medium egg yolk
2 tsp clear honey
crème fraîche or Greek yogurt,
   to serve

TASTY TIP

If fresh peaches are unavailable, use nectarines. Alternatively, use drained, tinned peach halves that have been packed in juice, rather than syrup. You can vary the filling according to personal preference – try ground almonds, caster sugar, crumbled trifle sponge cakes and lemon rind, moistened with medium sherry.

1 Preheat oven to 180°C/350°F/Gas Mark 4. Halve the peaches and remove the stones. Take a very thin slice from the bottom of each peach half so that it will sit flat on the baking sheet. Dip the peach halves in lemon juice and arrange on a baking sheet.

2 Crush the Amaretti biscuits lightly and put into a large bowl. Add the almonds, pine nuts, sugar, lemon zest and butter. Work with the fingertips until the mixture resembles coarse breadcrumbs. Add the egg yolk and mix well until the mixture is just binding.

3 Divide the Amaretti and nut mixture between the peach halves, pressing down lightly. Bake in the preheated oven for 15 minutes, or until the peaches are tender and the filling is golden. Remove from the oven and drizzle with the honey.

4 Place 2 peach halves on each serving plate and spoon over a little crème fraîche or Greek yogurt, then serve.

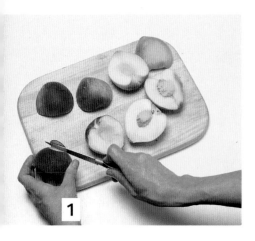

Almond & Pine Nut Tart

INGREDIENTS

Serves 4

250 g/9 oz ready-made sweet
   shortcrust pastry
75 g/3 oz blanched almonds
75 g/3 oz caster sugar
pinch of salt
2 medium eggs
1 tsp vanilla essence
2–3 drops almond essence
125 g/4 oz unsalted butter, softened
2 tbsp flour
½ tsp baking powder
3–4 tbsp raspberry jam
50 g/2 oz pine nuts
icing sugar, to decorate
whipped cream, to serve

TASTY TIP

Blend 175 g/6 oz plain flour and 75 g/3 oz cold butter in a food processor until it resembles coarse breadcrumbs. Add 25 g/1 oz caster sugar and blend briefly. Whisk 1 medium egg yolk with 2 tbsp of cold water and add to the mixture. Pulse until the mixture begins to form a ball. Tip on to a floured surface and knead until smooth. Wrap and refrigerate for 30 minutes.

1 Preheat oven to 200°C/400°F/Gas Mark 6. Roll out the pastry and use to line a 23 cm/9 inch fluted flan tin. Chill in the refrigerator for 10 minutes, then line with greaseproof paper and baking beans and bake blind in the preheated oven for 10 minutes. Remove the paper and beans and bake for a further 10–12 minutes until cooked. Leave to cool. Reduce the temperature to 190°C/375°F/Gas Mark 5.

2 Grind the almonds in a food processor until fine. Add the sugar, salt, eggs, vanilla and almond essence and blend. Add the butter, flour and baking powder and blend until smooth.

3 Spread a thick layer of the raspberry jam over the cooled pastry case, then pour in the almond filling. Sprinkle the pine nuts evenly over the top and bake for 30 minutes, until firm and browned.

4 Remove the tart from the oven and leave to cool. Dust generously with icing sugar and serve cut into wedges with whipped cream.

1

2

3

Coffee Ricotta

INGREDIENTS

Serves 6

700 g/1½ lb fresh ricotta cheese
125 ml/4 fl oz double cream
25 g/1 oz espresso beans,
  freshly ground
4 tbsp caster sugar
3 tbsp brandy
50 g/2 oz butter, softened
75 g/3 oz caster sugar
1 medium egg, beaten
50 g/2 oz plain flour

1 Preheat oven to 220°C/425°F/Gas Mark 7, 15 minutes before baking. Beat the ricotta and cream together until smooth. Stir in the ground coffee beans, sugar and brandy. Cover and refrigerate for at least 2 hours (the flavour improves the longer it stands). Meanwhile, oil 2 baking sheets and line with non-stick baking parchment.

2 Cream together the butter and sugar until fluffy. Gradually beat in the egg, a little at a time. In a bowl, sift the flour then fold into the butter mixture to form a soft dough. Spoon the mixture into a piping bag fitted with a 1 cm/½ inch plain nozzle. Pipe 7.5 cm/ 3 inch lengths of the mixture spaced well apart on to the baking sheet. Use a sharp knife to cut the dough off cleanly at the nozzle.

3 Bake in the preheated oven for 6–8 minutes, until just golden at the edges. Cool on the baking sheet for 5 minutes before transferring to a wire rack to cool completely.

4 To serve, spoon the coffee and ricotta mixture into small coffee cups. Serve with the biscuits.

HELPFUL HINT

When making the biscuits, spoon the mixture very carefully into the piping bag to avoid getting large air bubbles in the mixture. This will help to pipe the biscuits smoothly on to the baking sheet.

1

2

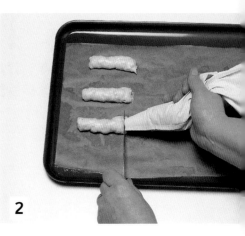

2

Zabaglione with Rum-soaked Raisin Compote

INGREDIENTS

Serves 6

2 tbsp raisins

1 strip thinly pared lemon zest

½ tsp ground cinnamon

3 tbsp Marsala wine

3 medium egg yolks

3 tbsp caster sugar

125 ml/4 fl oz dry white wine

150 ml/¼ pint double cream,
  lightly whipped

crisp biscuits, to serve

1 Put the raisins in a small bowl with the lemon zest and ground cinnamon. Pour over the Marsala wine to cover and leave to macerate for at least one hour. When the raisins are plump, lift out of the Marsala wine and reserve the raisins and wine, discarding the lemon zest.

2 In a large heatproof bowl, mix together the egg yolks and sugar. Add the white wine and Marsala wine and stir well to combine. Put the bowl over a saucepan of simmering water, ensuring that the bottom of the bowl does not touch the water. Whisk constantly until the mixture doubles in bulk.

3 Remove from the heat and continue whisking for about 5 minutes until the mixture has cooled slightly. Fold in the raisins and then immediately fold in the whipped cream. Spoon into dessert glasses or goblets and serve with crisp biscuits.

FOOD FACT

Zabaglione, an Italian concoction of eggs, sugar and wine is virtually identical to Sabayon – a French concoction of eggs, sugar and wine. Make the zabaglione as above and omit the raisins. Serve with poached pears, summer fruits or on its own in stemmed glasses.

1

2

3

Raspberry & Almond Tart

INGREDIENTS

Serves 6–8

For the pastry:
225 g/8 oz plain flour
pinch of salt
125 g/4 oz butter, cut into pieces
50 g/2 oz caster sugar
grated zest of ½ lemon
1 medium egg yolk

For the filling:
75 g/3 oz butter
75 g/3 oz caster sugar
75 g/3 oz ground almonds
2 medium eggs
225 g/8 oz raspberries, thawed
  if frozen
2 tbsp slivered or flaked almonds
icing sugar for dusting

1 Preheat oven to 200°C/400°F/Gas Mark 6, 15 minutes before cooking. Blend the flour, salt and butter in a food processor until the mixture resembles breadcrumbs. Add the sugar and lemon zest and blend again for 1 minute. Mix the egg yolk with 2 tablespoons of cold water and add to the mixture. Blend until the mixture starts to come together, adding a little more water if necessary, then tip out on to a lightly floured surface. Knead until smooth, wrap in clingfilm and chill in the refrigerator for 30 minutes.

2 Roll the dough out thinly on a lightly floured surface and use to line a 23 cm/9 inch fluted tart tin. Chill in the refrigerator for 10 minutes. Line the pastry case with greaseproof paper and baking beans. Bake for 10 minutes, then remove the paper and beans and return to the oven for a further 10–12 minutes until cooked. Allow to cool slightly, then reduce the oven temperature to 190°C/375°F/Gas Mark 5.

3 Blend together the butter, sugar, ground almonds and eggs until smooth. Spread the raspberries over the base of the pastry, then cover with the almond mixture. Bake for 15 minutes. Remove from the oven and sprinkle with the slivered or flaked almonds and dust generously with icing sugar. Bake for a further 15–20 minutes, until firm and golden brown. Leave to cool, then serve.

TASTY TIP
Omit the raspberries in the above tart. Spread the almond mixture over the base of the pastry case and top with poached or drained, tinned pear halves. Scatter over flaked almonds and bake as above.

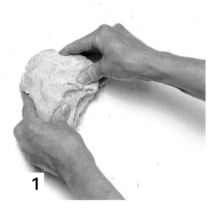

1

2

3

Goats' Cheese & Lemon Tart

INGREDIENTS

Serves 6–8

For the pastry:

125 g/4 oz butter, cut into
   small pieces
225 g/8 oz plain flour
pinch of salt
50 g/2 oz caster sugar
1 medium egg yolk

For the filling:

350 g/12 oz mild fresh goats'
   cheese, eg Chavroux
3 medium eggs, beaten
150 g/5 oz caster sugar
grated rind and juice of 3 lemons
450 ml/³/₄ pint double cream
fresh raspberries, to decorate
   and serve

1 Preheat oven to 200°C/400°F/Gas Mark 6, 15 minutes before cooking. Rub the butter into the plain flour and salt until the mixture resembles breadcrumbs, then stir in the sugar. Beat the egg yolk with 2 tablespoons of cold water and add to the mixture. Mix together until a dough is formed then turn the dough out on to a lightly floured surface and knead until smooth. Chill in the refrigerator for 30 minutes.

2 Roll the dough out thinly on a lightly floured surface and use to line a 4 cm/1¹/₂ inch deep 23 cm/9 inch fluted flan tin. Chill in the refrigerator for 10 minutes. Line the pastry case with greaseproof paper and baking beans or tinfoil and bake blind in the preheated oven for 10 minutes. Remove the paper and beans or tinfoil. Return to the oven for a further 12–15 minutes until cooked. Leave to cool slightly, then reduce the oven temperature to 150°C/300°F/ Gas Mark 2.

3 Beat the goats' cheese until smooth. Whisk in the eggs, sugar, lemon rind and juice. Add the cream and mix well.

4 Carefully pour the cheese mixture into the pastry case and return to the oven. Bake in the oven for 35–40 minutes, or until just set. If it begins to brown or swell, open the oven door for 2 minutes, then reduce the temperature to 120°C/250°F/Gas Mark ¹/₂ and leave the tart to cool in the oven. Chill in the refrigerator until cold. Decorate and serve with fresh raspberries.

TASTY TIP

The goat's cheese adds a certain unusual piquancy to this tart. Substitute full-fat soft cheese or ricotta, if preferred.

1

3

4

Tiramisu

INGREDIENTS

Serves 4

225 g/8 oz mascarpone cheese
25 g/1 oz icing sugar, sifted
150 ml/¼ pint strong brewed
  coffee, chilled
300 ml/½ pint double cream
3 tbsp coffee liqueur
125 g/4 oz Savoiardi or sponge
  finger biscuits
50 g/2 oz plain dark chocolate,
  grated or made into small curls
cocoa powder, for dusting
assorted summer berries, to serve

1 Lightly oil and line a 900 g/2 lb loaf tin with a piece of clingfilm. Put the mascarpone cheese and icing sugar into a large bowl and using a rubber spatula, beat until smooth. Stir in 2 tablespoons of chilled coffee and mix thoroughly.

2 Whip the cream with 1 tablespoon of the coffee liqueur until just thickened. Stir a spoonful of the whipped cream into the mascarpone mixture, then fold in the rest. Spoon half of the the mascarpone mixture into the prepared loaf tin and smooth the top.

3 Put the remaining coffee and coffee liqueur into a shallow dish just bigger than the biscuits. Using half of the biscuits, dip one side of each biscuit into the coffee mixture, then arrange on top of the mascarpone mixture in a single layer. Spoon the rest of the mascarpone mixture over the biscuits and smooth the top.

4 Dip the remaining biscuits in the coffee mixture and arrange on top of the mascarpone mixture. Drizzle with any remaining coffee mixture. Cover with clingfilm and chill in the refrigerator for 4 hours.

5 Carefully turn the tiramisu out on to a large serving plate and sprinkle with the grated chocolate or chocolate curls. Dust with cocoa powder, cut into slices and serve with a few summer berries.

FOOD FACT

This now classic Italian dessert appears in all kinds of forms in most Italian cookery books. The name literally means 'pick me up'.

1

2

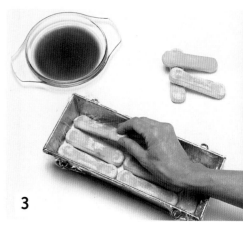

3

Cannoli with Ricotta Cheese

INGREDIENTS

Serves 24

For the pastry:
25 g/1 oz butter
25 g/1 oz caster sugar
3 tbsp dry white wine
pinch of salt
150 g/5 oz plain flour
1 medium egg, lightly beaten
vegetable oil, for deep frying

For the filling:
450 g/1 lb ricotta cheese
125 g/4 oz caster sugar
2 tbsp orange water
1 tsp vanilla essence
50 g/2 oz glacé cherries, chopped
50 g/2 oz angelica, chopped
125 g/4 oz candied peel, chopped
75 g/3 oz plain dark chocolate,
   finely chopped
icing sugar, for dusting

HELPFUL HINT
Cannoli moulds are difficult to come by outside Italy. Substitute cream horn moulds for lengths of 2.5 cm/1 inch thick bamboo or cane (washed thoroughly).

1 Beat together the butter and 25 g/1 oz of the sugar until light and fluffy. Add the white wine and salt and mix together well. Fold in the flour and knead to form a soft dough. Reserve for 2 hours.

2 Lightly flour a work surface and roll the dough out to a thickness of about ½ cm/¼ inch. Cut into 12.5 cm/5 inch squares. Wrap the pastry around the cannoli or cream horn moulds using the beaten egg to seal. Make 3–4 at a time.

3 Heat the vegetable oil to 180°C/350°F in a deep-fat fryer and fry the cannoli for 1–2 minutes, or until puffed and golden. Drain well on absorbent kitchen paper and leave to cool. Remove the moulds when the cannoli are cool enough to handle. Repeat until all the cannoli are cooked.

4 Beat the ricotta cheese with 125 g/4 oz of sugar, orange water and vanilla essence until creamy. Add the cherries, angelica, candied peel and chopped chocolate. Fill each cannoli using a piping bag with a large plain nozzle or a small spoon. Dust with icing sugar and serve cool, but not cold.

1

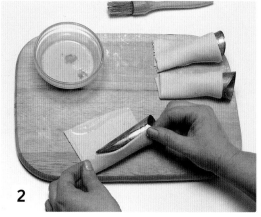

2

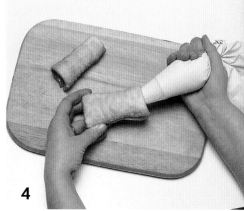

4

Index